London Confidential

Written by Michael Moynihan

Edited by Kathleen Peddicord

Agora Books
824 E. Baltimore St.
Baltimore, MD 21202

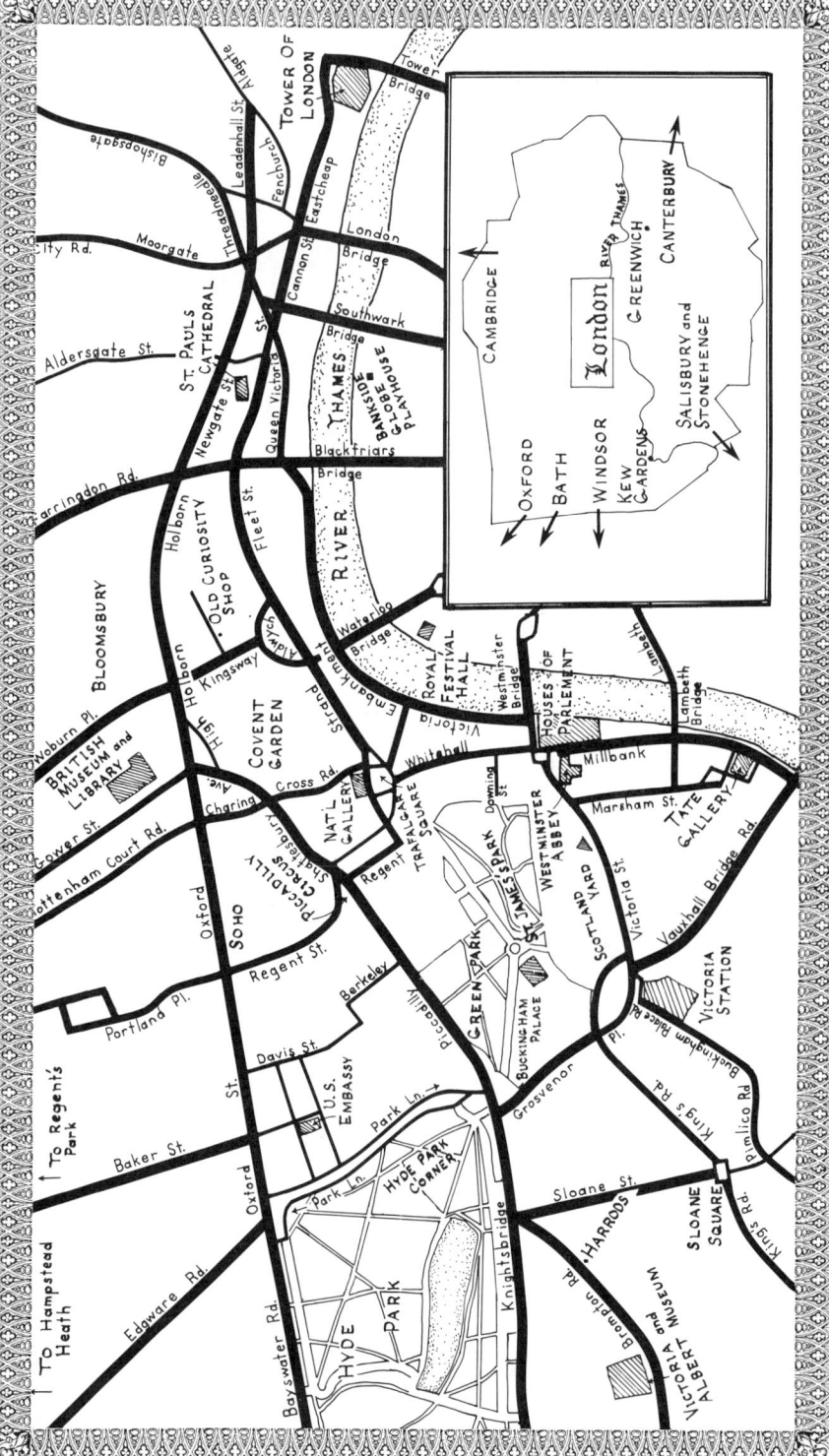

London Confidential

Written by Michael Moynihan

Publisher: William R. Bonner
Editorial Director: Vivian Lewis
Editor: Kathleen Peddicord
Managing Editor: Jane Lears
Production Manager: Becky Mangus
Interns: Jane Goode, Lynn Holden, and Deidre Mullervy
Cover Design: Jack French
Cover Photography: John Burwell

Copyright 1989 by Agora, Inc., 824 E. Baltimore St., Baltimore, MD 21202. All rights reserved. No part of this book may be reproduced in any form or by any means without written consent from the publisher.

ISBN: 0-945332-14-9

Table of Contents

Chapter I **1**
    Orientation 7
    Transportation to and from London 14
    Travel inside the city 17

Chapter II **23**
    Accommodations 29

Chapter III **39**
    Dining out 44

Chapter IV **59**
    Shopping 62

Chapter V **83**
    London's must-sees 93

Chapter VI **109**
    A night out in London 113

Chapter VII **123**
    London's pubs 129

Chapter VIII **133**
    Entertainment 139

Chapter IX **147**
    A bit of London's history 153

Chapter X **157**
    London's street markets 161

Chapter XI **163**
    Day trips from London 171

Chapter XII **179**

Index **181**

Chapter I

We all know London. Even before we visit the city, we know it from nursery rhymes, history books, and songs our mothers sang to us in the cradle. I will never lose certain childhood visions I have of this city—of bobbies dressed in blue, of beefeaters in red, of Mary Poppins holding a parasol, all wearing the funniest hats, all with glowing cheeks, and all from some long-forgotten storybook.

The British did well to develop such a brimming treasure of innocence, such a repertory of rhyme. You can get into trouble, all sorts of trouble, in London, but even Alice in Wonderland wakes up. Given England's history, that store of innocence serves her well. When all is said and done, you're back in a feather bed in the nursery, and it is time for tea. Remember Oliver, the poor urchin who was forced to pick pockets for Fagan but who found his wealthy relations in the end? Or Jane Eyre, who stumbled flu-ridden through the stormy heath but eventually found a cottage where relations offered tea before the fire?

As an American, I've always considered England a land of comforts, of that civilized life that America somehow missed. As though only a twist of plot led our country down the road of mass marketing and McDonald's and away from our national birthright. But a plane ticket can right all that, can take you not only to a different place but to a different life as well, to a life you might have lived—as a country squire with an interest in old phonographs, Japanese gardening, and polo, for example. Or as a cockney rake and gad about town. Or as a gentleman fond of old books, racing, and speculations on astrophysics. Oh for a ticket back to the land of well-cut leather shoes, tiny sandwiches, giant glasses of beer, and burled walnut umbrellas.

And so when my friend William Chamberlayne told me he needed someone to write a book about London, I had a momentary leap of the heart. I'm a journalist. And I've always had a love for that green land with red phones, gray skies, and black bowler hats.

At my age, I've written about every story a reporter can write—rewritten it, too—and I've my share of seniority. Why not, I thought, when I considered Chamberlayne's offer? I met Bill Bonner (Chamberlayne's publisher) at the Oyster Bar of the Plaza when he came through New York on business. We hit it off quite famously over some wine and Chesapeake oysters—which Bill obligingly paid for. We talked about our mutual friend William Chamberlayne, then Bill mentioned an advance and a figure for expenses. The deal was made as far as I was concerned—though I hemmed and hawed a bit.

My paper in New York gave me a leave of absence. The next thing I knew I had deposited Bill's checks, arranged for a young woman studying animal medicine to take care of Jason, my collie, found a visiting Chinese professor at Columbia to sublet my apartment (he promised to water my papyrus), packed lightly, and caught an autumn evening cab, complete with a Russian cabby who hated his job. "Three years I am cab slave. Save money? No, you can't save money as cab slave," the driver complained.

I boarded British Air to London. Agora (Bonner's publishing company) had booked me a full economy seat, but I used an old trick I know to get an upgrade—I simply asked. If they have empty seats, most airlines will let you move up to business or first class, as long as you've paid full-fare. I felt like I'd won the lottery. I must have looked like it, too, because everyone who saw me smiled. The champagne and British Air beluga added to my overall feeling of contentment—as did the friendly stewardess wearing a bobby's hat and a warm smile and the soothing classical music. I half expected Cristopher Morley to come out from behind a screen and toast me with, "You deserve it, old boy."

I've spent plenty of time in London over the years, on one job or another. I've always enjoyed the city. It offers just what you need for a break. Empire and all that and....yes, I'll take another glass of that cognac and a Havana cigar.

When you arrive in quiet Heathrow airport, you're struck by its English pragmatism. No wild French futurism as at Charles De Gaulle, no German hyper-efficiency. A bit chaotic, sure. But no detours because of construction, no endless plywood tunnels, no hustlers looking for tourists, no taxi horns, no sirens like those I'd left in New York.

We had the good luck to beat the flight from Cairo to immigration. In the past, I've watched kindly British inspectors turn into deans of orphanages, greeting each new arrival with a stinging boxing of the ears. But we were through in 10 minutes. Outside customs I found banks ready to change my money, along with a service ready to book me a room—but I already had one— at the Ritz. At my age, I like to do these things in advance, and I like my comforts.

If you want to get from Heathrow to downtown, you have three options: the tube, the airbus, or a taxi. At about £2, the tube (the Piccadilly line) is the least expensive alternative; the cab, which costs about £20, is the most expensive. At £4, the airbus seemed the right choice. I took the A1 bus to Hyde Park Corner, the stop nearest the Ritz (the A2 goes to Euston Station). Groups will make out better by cab, as will people traveling alone at odd hours or to unusual destinations. But the bus saved me £16. If only I could lose that much weight.

For about an hour my bus negotiated its way past scores of little houses, all neat and multi-chimneyed. England has more chimneys than any other country on earth. More brick, too. Driving through the country you can't help but picture couples having tea before a fire. A country of hearthside comforts.

London, looking north toward the Strand.

I craned my neck at the first real pub. And then the city. Brompton Road, with the Victoria and Albert Museum, the fairytale splendor of Harrods (now owned by Egyptians), Knightsbridge, Hyde Park Corner. I had told the driver of the doubledecker bus my destination, so he idled the motor and walked out into the street to hail me a cab. A tip would have been out of place.

It was morning in London, but once I was inside the revolving doors of the Ritz, all traffic noises disappeared. I felt I'd walked back a century. I trod over thick carpets beneath large chandeliers to the reception desk, where a matronly lady told me Nelson would take my bags. The ancient Nelson appeared, smiling approvingly. "Traveling light, sir. Oh, yes. Very good."

The Ritz.

Upstairs my footman opened a window and placed my bag on a stand. I took some time to look out the window at the cloudy but brilliant sky over sublime Green Park. (The park is so-named because flowers are banned from it. It seems the king was caught picking flowers here for his mistress, and the queen didn't approve.) The clouds were playing cat and mouse with the sun. I noticed the writing desk—all set up for one like me, with a fine bonded leather blotter and rich, layered papers. Yes, the ghost of César Ritz is still alive on Piccadilly—César Ritz, who made the Savoy a great hotel as well. And then I took a nap.

When I first arrived in London, I had no idea that this trip would turn out to be one of the strangest adventures of my life. You never know what will happen when you travel. But the experienced traveler realizes that a trip often can take you places you'd never dreamed of, much less planned for.

On this trip, I was to find myself caught in a web of people and events that I did not understand. It was as if I were one of Hitchcock's most unsuspecting characters, involved in a complex tale of deception and intrigue. The American man and the foreign strangers, connected by the invisible threads of some underhanded plot, like a connect-the-dot puzzle with a sinister message.

At first, I attributed my unease and the feeling of being followed to the strangeness of being in London. It had been many years since I'd been in the city, and it has changed. I noticed fewer gentlemen and more skinheads. A disconcerting thought. But I shrugged off my feelings of discomfort and tried to concentrate on my purpose: gathering information for this book.

I rose at noon—against the will of every cell in my body—

took a hot shower (which did wonders for my jet lag), sampled the huge, thick towels, and resolved to do some sightseeing. I chose a blue English suit from H. Huntsman that still fit me after all these years (no need to accentuate the gray of the sky), a pink shirt, and a red paisley tie. British tailors have a respect for age that others would do well to emulate.

After I'd dressed, I called a number that William Chamberlayne had mentioned. A Ms. Jenny Wilde, giver of private tours.

The voice on the other end was quite cheery and English. "Yes, I'm leading a small tour this afternoon at the British Museum if you'd care to join us. No queues. Just meet across the street in front of the Museum Tavern. You're working on a guidebook?"

"That's right." I was suddenly aware of my New York drawl. "I'm here for a few months, and I want to see the sights. I know London, but it changes so fast."

"It certainly does that, Mr...."

"Woods. John Woods."

"We have the same initials, don't we Mr. Woods? Very well, I'll look for you at 2 p.m. I'll be wearing a red jacket and carrying a red brollie. Blond hair. Red brollie. I think you'll like the group. You'll be joining a sheik or two and an eccentric Japanese."

"Really?" I asked.

"That's right. Tag," she answered. Click.

I went downstairs to look for the bar. In addition to its small bar (the old splendid one is gone), the Ritz has a wonderful dining room facing the park. And the Palm Court, where you can have tea, has some of the most elegant palms in London. I decided to eat. As a guest of the hotel, Vincent, the maitre d', was able to squeeze me in, even though reservations are usually required. I was stuck away from the windows, but the room was quite cheery; with its trompe l'oeil ceiling, it is recognized as the prettiest dining room in England. Outside, the sky was a brilliant white.

The Ritz, like many fine London eateries, offers a *prix-fixe* menu for lunch that is a steal. For £17.50, including service and tax, liveried servants brought me a salad of smoked chicken and duck in a sherry and mango dressing. This was followed by a sumptuous veal filet glazed with cheese and served on noodles. A

The Palm Court at the Ritz.

half-bottle of red wine brought the bill to just under £25. Not cheap, but not bad. Nothing relieves jet lag faster than eating and drinking, particularly drinking—I learned that long ago.

Outside, the sun had made an appearance. A man sporting the height of 18th-century livery ran into the street to hail me a cab, and I took a trip through history: the great Victorian buildings of Piccadilly; the majesty of gently curving Regent Street; the neoclassicism of Piccadilly Circus; and the raging commerce of Haymarket. I looked out at Burberrys, American Express, and the royal profusion of Her Majesty's, where *The Phantom of the Opera* was playing. Trafalgar Square, the world capital of pigeons paying court to Admiral Nelson. All the trappings of an empire on which the sun had decided to smile.

It felt good to ride in an English cab again. All that room to put up your feet, a trusted driver, the assurance of a well-regulated system, and yards of black, gleaming paint. Near Charing Cross, we got caught in a traffic jam, just as the sun set behind the clouds.

"What's this?" I asked.

"Don't know. Some commotion, likely," said the cockney driver. "Must be important, though." I heard piercing European sirens.

"How's that?"

"MI5. There." He pointed to members of the British secret service patroling the street. Then he made an amazing pinpoint U-turn.

"Nicely done," I murmured, quite impressed.

"Yes sir," he piped. He took us an odd route. My eyes were still thrilling to all the Victorian turrets and turns, the elegant Georgian facades. Those first few hours in a foreign city. The smell in the air was distinctly European—of diesel, not petrol.

A bit later we pulled up in front of the British Museum. I got out and paid the driver through the window (I included a tip of 15%). Across the street stood a tall, well-dressed woman with blond hair. Even from my distant vantage point I could see her blue eyes. She was holding a red umbrella. When I began to walk toward her, she seemed to recognize me and jerked the umbrella up. I nodded.

"Mr. Woods?"

"Yes."

"Welcome to London. Are you ready?"

"Aren't we waiting for some others?"

"No, I'm afraid they canceled. It's just us. Just us two. C'mon," she said.

And we crossed to the museum.

*   *   *

Before I begin to describe my trip to the museum, I'd like to give you some general information that I hope will prove useful when you first arrive in London. I'd rather get the mundane out of the way, so I'll begin with the basics: currency, electric current, tipping, telephones, telegrams, the postal service, and the like. Then I'll fill you in on how to get to London and how to get around the city once you're there.

Orientation

Currency

If you have American Express traveler's checks, cash them (free of charge) at an **American Express** office. The main branch, *6 Haymarket; tel. 930-4411; tube: Piccadilly,* is open Monday through Friday from 9 a.m. to 5 p.m.; Saturday from 9 a.m. to 6 p.m. (it remains open on Saturday until 8 p.m. from June through September); Sunday from 10 a.m. to 6 p.m. Other offices are located at *147 Victoria St.; tel. 828-7411; 52 Cannon St.;*

tel. 248-2671; tube: Cannon Street; 82 Brompton Road; tel. 584-6182, across the street from Harrods; *tube: Knightsbridge;* and in the **British Travel Center,** *12 Regent St.; tel. 839-2682.*

Because Barclay's sells its own checks, it charges a minimum commission of £3, plus a percentage, to cash American Express checks. For $50 worth of checks, that comes to about 10%. However, Barclay's cashes its own checks for free and, along with National Westminster and Midlands, offers the best rates on cash.

Consider Thomas Cook only if you have Thomas Cook checks or can't get to an American Express office or a bank. The Thomas Cook office outside Victoria Station is open from 6 a.m. to 10 p.m. Berkeley Safe Deposit outside Victoria Station is open from 8 a.m. to midnight. The Trafalgar Square Post Office changes currency Monday through Saturday from 9 a.m. to 9:30 p.m.—at a hefty commission. If at all possible, avoid all the Bureaux de Change, which charge a commission of about 10%.

I have no great love of technology, but I have to admit that it can be handy—especially for an inveterate carouser like myself. I've made more than one late-night stop at the American Express Automatic Teller Machine (ATM) on *Haymarket Street* (others are located in the forecourt of Victoria Station facing the cab queue and at *82 Brompton Road*). At these machines, my American Express card gets me pounds at a rate well below that of the long-fingered Bureaux de Change. To use the machines, you must be enrolled in American Express' Express Cash service (the money you withdraw from the machine is deducted from your account).

Visa cards also work in many ATM machines, but you must pay interest on the money you withdraw. And during daylight hours, American Express card holders can cash personal checks into pounds free of charge.

Citibank card holders with the word "Link" marked on their cards probably have the best deal of all. They can get pounds any time at any ATM also marked with the word "Link"—these include ATMs of Abbey National and many other building societies (which are similar to U.S. thrifts). Charges may apply.

Check with your bank to see if it's a member of any network operating in London. Undoubtedly, other banks soon will follow Citibank's lead.

Electric current

The current in England is 240 volts AC, 50 to 60 cycles. New sockets have three large prongs; old ones (which are almost gone) have two round prongs. Electric shavers can be plugged directly into the wall if you use a fused adaptor (U.S. to English), available at hardware stores and Radio Shack. Some hotels have U.S.-style plugs that can be used for shavers *only*. Do not plug anything else from the United States into a wall socket without using a transformer that converts 110 volts to 240 volts. Buy the transformer (usually a bulky, expensive object) in the United States if possible.

It is generally unwise to buy anything electric in England (to take back to the United States), although some lights without fuses may be transportable. If you do buy something electric in England, you'll find that the English don't make their appliances with plugs already attached. You must attach them yourself.

Tipping

Give 10% to 15% to cab drivers and waiters (when the service is not included on the bill). A small tip is appreciated by porters, doormen, and hairdressers.

Telephones

London's recently privatized telephone system, British Telecom (which is undergoing modernization), offers reliable, if expensive, service throughout the United Kingdom.

The country code for England is *44;* the city code for London is *01*. To make a direct-dial international call from London, dial *010,* the country

The Bayswater Omnibus *by G.W. Joy.*

code (*1* for the United States), then the area code and number. Dial *100* for the operator, *155* for the international operator. Directory assistance is *142* for London, *192* for the rest of Britain, and *153* for international numbers.

Most hotels charge an exorbitant markup on international calls—check with the management. An alternative is to make international calls from a telephone office (one is located at *1 Broadway; tube: St. James's Park*). Or, armed with a lot of change, a Phone Card (which is described below), or a credit card, try calling from a payphone. Another alternative, which may be your best bet, is to dial *0800-8900-11*. This gets you the AT&T operator back in the United States, who can bill calls to your home (if someone is there to OK it) or to your AT&T credit card number.

London has two types of payphones. The most common accepts coins of 2p, 5p, 10p, 50p, and £1 (in any denomination but 1p) and has an LED screen to tell you how much you've put in. To place a call, lift the receiver, put in the sufficient amount of money (in small coins), and dial. Inside London, 20p (one 10p piece and two 5p pieces, for example) will do for a short call. Remember, Londoners do not gab on the telephone like we do. They can't afford to. A U.S.-style three-minute call costs a bundle.

A continuous tone (or brrr) is the dial tone; an intermittent brrr means the phone is ringing; a shrill squeal means you've reached a non-working number; a quick repeating tone means the line is engaged.

At the end of your call, unused coins—but not change—are returned (hence the logic of using small coins).

London's older type of payphone, now all but extinct, also uses coins, but it has no LED. Lift the receiver and dial. When your party answers, a series of pips commences. Deposit the appropriate money; if the pips resume during your conversation, you must deposit more money (you have 15 seconds after the pips begin to pay up or scream your goodbye).

To save yourself this indecency, I strongly recommend that you get a Phone Card. These bright green credit card-sized inventions are available in denominations of £1, £2, £4, and £10 at post offices, stores, and hotels. When you insert your card, the telephone will tell you how many units you have remaining. Simply dial and converse; units are subtracted automatically. When making several calls in succession, use the small button marked "Follow up" to avoid the long wait for a dial tone. Remember to retrieve your card when you're finished. Cards have a bad habit of lingering a few seconds before popping out—just long enough to let you forget them.

A few telephones at airports accept credit cards. But these phones are almost never on hand when you need one.

Most international calls are cheapest Monday through Friday from 8 p.m. to 8 a.m. and on weekends. (However, the cheapest times to call Australia are midnight to 7 a.m. and 2:30 p.m. to 7 p.m.) Calls inside Britain are most expensive Monday through Friday from 9 a.m. to 1 p.m., less expensive from 1 p.m. to 6 p.m., and least expensive from 6 p.m. to 9 a.m. and on weekends.

The following telephone numbers might prove useful when traveling through Britain:

- **Time,** *123* (London only).
- **Traffic,** *246-8021.*
- **Weather,** *246-8091.*
- **Business news,** *246-8026.*

Telegrams

To send an international telegram, dial *193*. For international telegram information, dial *197*. For telemessages, dial *190*.

The postal service

London's best post office (it's open the latest) is the **Trafalgar Square Post Office,** *24-28 William IV St. (corner of St. Martin's Lane); tel. 930-9580.* It is open Monday through Saturday from 8 a.m. to 8 p.m.; Sunday and holidays from 10 a.m. to 5 p.m.

Friends can address *poste restante* mail to you at any post office you specify. To pick up mail at the main office, have it addressed to you as follows: *Poste Restante, Trafalgar Square Post Office, London WC2N 4DL.* Unaddressed mail goes to the **London Chief Office,** *King Edward Building; tel. 239-5049; tube: St. Pauls.* This branch is open Monday through Friday from 8 a.m. to 7 p.m.; Saturday from 9 a.m. to 12:30 p.m. American Express will hold mail for 30 days at any office. This service is free to card holders, but others must pay a fee.

Federal Express

Many courier companies operate in London, but I like **Federal Express,** because it allows me to charge to my U.S. account. Although Federal Express doesn't have an office in downtown London, it will pick up anywhere. Call before 4 p.m. for same-day pickup. London numbers include *594-9811, 890-4955, 844-2226,* and *622-3933.*

If you're sending anything but documents overseas, you must fill out an invoice form (which Federal Express will explain).

Emergency information

In case of an emergency, dial *999* (the call is free). This connects you with the police, the fire department, and medical assistance.

An emergency room in England is called a casualty ward. Hospitals with casualty wards include:

- **Middlesex Hospital,** *Mortimer Street; tel. 636-8333.*
- **St. Mary's Hospital,** *Praed Street; tel. 262-1280.*
- **St. Thomas' Hospital,** *Lambeth Palace Road; tel. 928-9292.*

During an emergency, hospitals must treat you free of charge, regardless of your citizenship. Once the emergency has passed, however, non-citizens must pay for care. Hospitals generally accept insurance if you're covered—which, of course, depends on your policy.

Local police keep lists of nearby doctors and chemists for emergencies.

Good drugstores open late include **Boots,** *tel. 734-6126,* on the northeast side of Piccadilly Circus (open Monday through Saturday from 9 a.m. to 8 p.m.), and **Bliss Chemists,** *55-56 Wilesden Lane; tel. 624-8000; tube: Kilburn* (open to 11 p.m.; the prescription service is open 24 hours a day).

London's **police headquarters,** *Broadway and Victoria streets; tel. 230-1212,* known as New Scotland Yard, is open 24 hours a day.

The **Samaritans,** *3 Morton Place; tel. 283-3400,* are well-respected for helping people in the midst of emotional crises. Call the 24-hour hotline if you need to talk through a problem.

The Rape Crisis Line of the **London Rape Crisis Centre,** *tel. 837-1600,* is open 24 hours for women who have been sexually assaulted. Women are encouraged to call for information or just to talk.

Transportation for the disabled can be arranged through the **Federation of London Dial-a-Ride,** *tel. 482-2325.*

For legal release, contact **Release,** *1 Elgin Ave.; tel. 289-1123; tube: Westbourne Park.* You can reach the 24-hour hotline by calling *837-5602* or *603-8654.*

The **Capital Help Line,** *tel. 388-7575,* provides all-around referrals.

Embassies and high commissions

The following embassies and high commissions are closed on English holidays:

- **Australia High Commission,** *Australia House, the Strand; tel. 438-8000; tube: Aldwych or Charing Cross.*

- **Canadian High Commission,** *Canada House, Trafalgar Square; tel. 692-9492; tube: Charing Cross* (open Monday through Friday from 9 a.m. to 5 p.m.; the telephone is answered 24 hours a day).
- **Irish Embassy,** *17 Grosvenor Place; tel. 235-2171; tube: Hyde Park Corner.*
- **New Zealand High Commission,** *New Zealand House, the Haymarket at Pall Mall; tel. 839-4580; tube: Charing Cross.*
- **United States Embassy,** *24 Grosvenor Square; tel. 499-9000* (open Monday through Friday from 9 a.m. to 5:30 p.m.; the telephone is answered 24 hours a day, but little can be done nights and after 3 p.m. Saturday, until the embassy opens again).

Travel information

The **Tourist Information Centre,** *forecourt of Victoria Station; tel. 730-3488,* is crowded but reasonably well-run. It distributes information, books hotel rooms (for £3), sells theater tickets, changes currency (for a price), and sells travel books. The bureau is open daily from 9 a.m. to 8:30 p.m. (the bookstore closes at 8 p.m. from April through October, at 6 p.m. from November through March). Smaller tourist information bureaus are located at Heathrow Airport, the Tower of London (West Gate; open during the summer only), Harrods (fourth floor), and Selfridges (ground floor).

The **British Travel Center,** *12 Regent St.; tel. 730-3400; tube: Piccadilly* (open Monday through Friday from 9 a.m. to 6:30 p.m.;

Saturday and Sunday from 10 a.m. to 4 p.m.), is a well-run pavilion that houses an American Express office, a British Rail office, a free travel information service, a theater ticket agency, an accommodation service, a well-stocked travel bookstore, travel agents, and other services for travelers. This is a great place to go for general travel information—although it can be crowded in the summer.

Teletourist, *tel. 246-8041,* provides information on events planned each day. **London for Children,** *tel. 246-8007,* gives recorded information concerning events of interest to children.

Transportation to and from London

Travel by air

London has two major airports: **Heathrow,** *tel. 759-4321; tube: Piccadilly* (a long walk from Terminal 3), and **Gatwick,** *tel. 668-4211.* In addition, a commuter airport is located in the Docklands, and **Stansted Airport,** *tel. 0279-502-380,* lies one hour north of the city, in Essex. Most major airlines use Heathrow, which consists of four terminals. British Air dominates Terminal 4, but no hard rules dictate which airlines leave or arrive from where. Charters generally use Gatwick.

Heathrow Airport is 16 miles from the city. A taxi downtown costs about £16 to £23. The **airbus** (there are two: A1 to Victoria Station and A2 to Euston), *tel. 222-1234,* departs every 20 to 30 minutes between 6:10 a.m. and some time after 9 p.m. (the time of the last bus depends on the route) and takes up to 60 minutes. The cost is £4, £2 for children.

Gatwick Airport is 30 miles south of London. A taxi downtown costs £40 and is not the recommended way to get to the city. British Rail gets you to Victoria Station in 45 minutes. The cost is £4.50. The **Green Line** bus, *tel. 668-7261,* travels to Victoria Station in 70 minutes. Take Coach Number 777, which departs every half-hour from 7 a.m. to 6 p.m. The cost is £3.

Buses departing Stansted Airport for London are timed to follow the schedules of arriving flights. The cost is £3.

Train travel

Although London has eight major train stations, most international trains come and go from Victoria.

For information on getting to London by train, contact the following stations:

• **Charing Cross Station,** *tel. 928-5100* (for trains to and from France and the south).

• **Euston Station,** *tel. 387-7070* or *387-9400* (for trains to and from Ireland, the North Midlands, northern Wales, the northwest, and Scotland, including Glasgow, by way of the west coast).

• **King's Cross Station,** *tel. 278-2477* or *837-4200* (for trains to and from the east, the northeast, and Scotland, including Edinburgh, by way of the east coast).

• **Liverpool Street Station,** *tel. 283-7171* or *247-7600* (for trains to and from Scandinavia, Essex, and East Anglia).

• **Paddington Station,** *tel. 262-6767* or *723-7000* (for trains to and from the west, the southwest, the South Midlands, and southern Wales).

• **St. Pancras Station,** *tel. 387-7070* or *387-9400* (for trains to and from the North Midlands).

• **Victoria Station,** *tel. 928-5100* (for trains to and from France, Scandinavia, the south, the southeast, and Gatwick Airport).

• **Waterloo Station,** *tel. 928-5100* (for trains to and from the south and the southeast).

Travel by bus (or coach)

The main coach station is **Victoria Coach Station,** *124 Buckingham Palace Road; tel. 730-0202,* two blocks south of Victoria Station. Areas close to London are served by Green Line buses (for more information on these buses, inquire at the kiosk behind the station on Eccleston Bridge, *tel. 668-7261;* it is open daily from 8:30 a.m. to 5:30 p.m.).

Green Line offers many discount plans, including the one-day Golden Rover ticket (£3.95, £2 for children); the discounted Outback one-day return ticket (up to 50% off); the seven-day Rover ticket (£12.50, £6.25 for children); and the one-year Faresaver Card, which allows half-price travel for those under 24 (£3; a photo is required). All these discounted tickets are subject to time and route restrictions—check with Green Line.

If you are in a hurry, take a National Express bus (which run from Victoria Coach Station). Green Line buses are slower and make more stops.

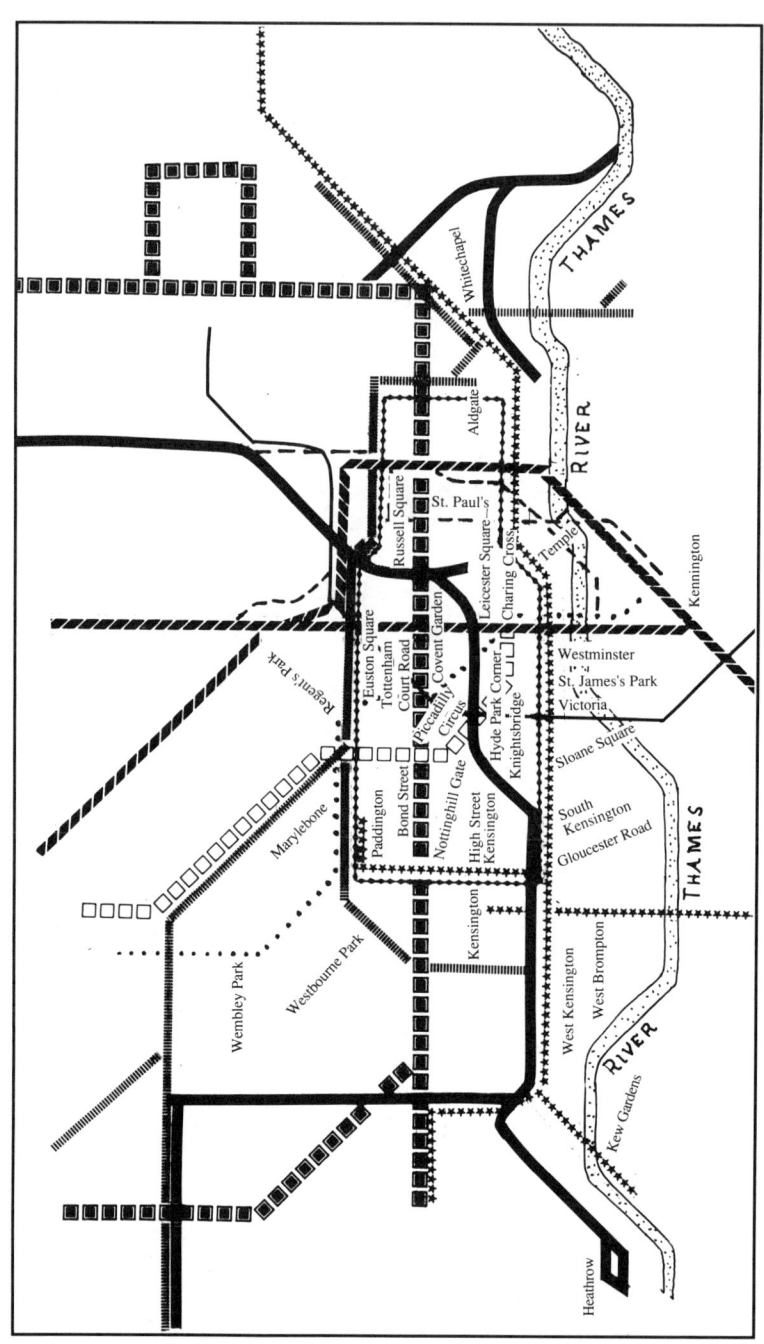

Travel by ferry

Sealink, *tel. 834-8122,* operates car ferries from Dover and New Haven to Calais and Boulogne (£14 one way, £55 for a car, and £66 for a car and one person) and to Dieppe (£19 one way, £52 for a car, and £68 for a car and one person). Offices are located in Victoria Station near Platform 2, *tel. 834-2345* (open daily from 8 a.m. to 6 p.m.; same-day service is available Saturday only) and in other major rail stations.

Travel inside the city

The underground (or the tube)

"Good afternoon, this is London Transport Information Central. Well, it's been one of those days on the Northern Line. We had a couple of signal problems this morning, and these have predictably snowballed," begins the recording. London has an extensive underground rail network, aptly known as the tube. The recording above illustrates the two sides of the system. On the one hand, service has deteriorated during the last few years due to the government's policy of promoting automobiles over public transport. More surface traffic has driven bus riders to the tube, prompting newspapers to complain about "tubular hell."

On the other hand, the underground services a huge area and still provides the quickest transport in town. And blackboard signs and recordings offer genuine apologies for the frequent delays, trash fires, and other difficulties—a far cry from the situation in New York. And the upholstered cars are comfortable (although tall riders like me will find the round design of the older lines allows us to stand only in the middle of the car). But you should avoid the quite uncivilized crush of rush hour.

Trains run from 5:30 a.m. to midnight (11:30 p.m. on Sunday)—although you might be able to catch one later. And if you make one late train, you can be pretty sure (but not positive) you will make your connection. The atmosphere of the tube after the pubs close is quite jolly. You may be regaled by singing drunks or comedians. If you miss the last tube, take a night bus (see "Buses" below).

Trips in the large central zone, roughly bounded by the Circle Line, cost 50p. Otherwise, ticket prices depend on how many zones you cross—check the schedule in the station. You can purchase underground tickets at a window or from a machine. Be sure to keep your ticket with you. No one will look at it when you enter, but you must hand it over to the guard when you exit. These apparently bored but in fact eagle-eyed souls almost never miss a ticket and can instantly tell if you paid the proper fare.

If you have underestimated your fare, go to an Excess Fare window before trying to exit. Always buy a ticket—fare fiddling is severely frowned upon and punished.

The nearby Thames River and the city's great rainfall dictated that the tubes be run far underground. Because they are so far belowground, many stations have elevators to take you down into the earth and back up again. Take my advice: If a station has an elevator, use it. Don't take the stairs. Some of these stations are so deep that they were used as bomb shelters during World War II, and the spiral stairs are dizzying. (Hampstead is the deepest station. Covent Garden, the second-deepest station, is haunted by the ghost of a stabbed tragedian.)

Even the escalators in these stations are giant. In 1911, London Transport introduced the first escalators at Earl's Court. A wooden-legged man named Bumper Harris was hired to ride up and down all day to demonstrate the new convenience.

Many connections strain the definition with endless climbs, descents, and marches, a problem for those with baggage.

Pay attention to destinations, because some lines split up outside the center of the city. This is particularly true of the vexing District and Circle lines. (These lines, however, have larger cars.)

Many stations have displays to tell you how many minutes before the next train. Destinations appear on the front of the trains and on the displays—but not on individual cars. You may have to push a button on the door of the train to make it open.

If you're planning to be in London for a while, purchase a Travel Card. These are available for one day (£2, £1 for children), seven days, or longer. The seven-day pass for one zone (inner London) costs £5.40; I recommend getting the pass for two zones (£6.90), which includes all but outer London. You'll need a passport photo (available from booths in the underground; four photos cost £1).

The Travel Card allows unlimited travel on the tube, the bus, and Docklands Light Railway within appropriate zones. If you purchase an annual Travel Card and return it, you can receive a refund for time remaining.

The Explorer Pass for tourists (seven days for £11.50) has little to recommend it.

British Rail

Where the tube fears to tread, British Rail will take you. In particular, British Rail services much of the South Bank at prices comparable to those for the tube.

If you plan to commute frequently by British Rail, invest in a Capital Card (comparable to a Travel Card). It offers unlimited tube, bus, and British Rail transport near London but cannot be used for long hauls upcountry. A one-day Capital Card costs £3 (the Capital 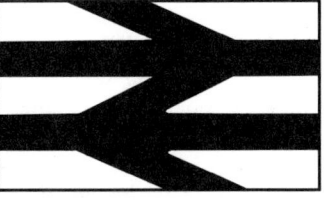 Card generally costs 30p to 80p more than a comparable Travel Card). Cards for children are less than half-price.

Buses

London has an extensive, if complicated, bus network. Double-decker buses are fun, British, even regal, and they offer great views of the city. Remember, though, that buses are slow, often intolerably so at rush hour.

You can get a free map of bus routes at any underground station. Or you can examine the route maps at bus stops. If you're in no particular hurry, simply board a bus and see where it goes.

At the bus stop, take your place in the queue (the driver may not let everyone on). When you board, tell the driver your destination, and he will tell you how much you owe. (On buses with an open rear platform, you can take a seat and wait for the conductor to approach. He will ask you your destination, tell you the fare, and, if you ask, alert you to your stop.) Single-decker Red Arrow buses run express and charge a flat fee. You can request a stop by ringing the bell.

Buses run from 6 a.m. to midnight. After midnight, you can catch a night bus. These run less frequently on routes marked with an "N." Trafalgar Square is a good place to catch a night bus, but you also can catch them on Oxford Street and at Victoria and King's Cross stations.

The Travel Card, described above, allows unlimited travel on the city's bus system. Also available are one-day bus passes (£2).

The basic fare for taking the bus in central London is 50p. If you cross zones, the fare goes up accordingly.

Taxis

London taxis are perhaps the finest in the world. Drivers, who are carefully regulated, know the city like the proverbial backs of their hands. To get his license, a driver must know how to reach any destination within a 20-mile radius of London. He is required to take you anywhere within six miles of where you hail him. And the cabs, besides offering charm, are

19

designed as cabs. They can turn on a dime and are easy to get in and out of. Fold-up seats allow groups to converse politely.

A cab is available if its yellow light is on. For trips of less than six miles, the driver must use the meter, but for long hauls, you and he agree on a price. If your bag is placed in the front of the cab (dispatchers tend to put bags there at stations), you must pay extra; however, if you keep your luggage in the back seat with you, you pay no extra charge. If you call for a cab, the driver will start the meter from wherever he is. When you reach your destination, get out of the cab first, then pay the driver through the window.

Downtown, cabs leave from **Russell Square,** *tel. 636-1247,* **Sloane Square,** *tel. 730-2664,* **Baker Street tube,** *tel. 935-2553,* and **St. George's Square,** *tel. 834-1014.* To call for a cab downtown, you also can try *286-4848, 272-3030, 286-6128, 286-6010,* or *286-1046.*

If you lose something in a taxi, contact the **Lost Property Office,** *15 Penton St., Islington; tel. 278-1744; tube: Angel* (open Monday through Friday).

In addition to the city's regular cabs, you'll see unlicensed minicabs, which consist of a man and a car at a stand. These stands, which are manned by dispatchers, dot the West End. Although police counsel against minicabs, which have a bad reputation, queues form at the stands after the pubs close. If you take one of these, always agree on a fare before you get in.

Late at night regular cabs collect on the Piccadilly side of Leicester Square, where drivers grab a cuppa (tea) and read the paper. If stranded, wander over here, ask about, and you'll soon have a ride.

Driving in the city

Although England is great for rallies and touring, London is a miserable place to drive. The distances are long, the one-way streets unpredictable, and the traffic often galling. Downtown, the speed limit is 30 mph (48 kph), unless otherwise marked. Seat belts are required. Pedestrians have the right of way, unless you have a green light. Horns are illegal after 11:30 p.m. And, of course, you must drive on the left.

Car parks in town charge about £2 to £3 for an hour, £5 to £7.50 for six hours. Near Piccadilly, try the car park at *Brewer Street; tel. 731-9497;* near Tower Hill, try the one on *Lower Thames Street; tel. 626-2082;* in Bedfordbury, try the car park at *48 St. Martin's Lane.*

You can park on the street, but beware the clamp, which immobilizes your wheels and costs a great deal to remove. You cannot park in areas marked with two yellow lines; areas marked with one yellow line are off-limits Monday through Saturday from 8 a.m. to 6:30 p.m. In addition, look for signs restricting the length of your stay or stipulating residents only.

Gasoline, called petrol, is sold by the liter. It takes 4.5 of these Napoleonic measures to make up the imperial gallon. Most pumps are self-serve.

If all this isn't enough to dissuade you from wanting to drive in London, you can rent a car from **Hertz Rental Car,** *Radnor House, 1272 London Road; tel. 679-1799;* **Avis Rental Car,** *35 Headfort Place; tel. 245-9862* (for reservations anywhere in London); and **National Rental Car,** *Trident House, Station Road, Hayes, Middlesex; tel. 848-8733* (for reservations worldwide, dialing from London).

The *New York Times* recently reported that **Budget Rent A Car,** *tel. 441-5882,* provides the cheapest rates of the major car-rental companies.

Mopeds and motorcycles

To rent a moped or a motorcycle, go to **Scootabout Limited,** *59 Albert Embankment; tel. 582-0055; tube: Vauxhall.* Mopeds cost £10.95 per day, £7.80 per day on a weekly basis. To rent a motorcycle, you need a deposit and a valid motorcycle driver's license.

Bicycles

If you wish to peddle your way around London, you can rent a bicycle from **Chelsea Cycles,** *13-15 Park; tel. 352-3999;* **Dial-A-Bike,** *18 Gillingham St.; tel. 828-4040;* or **On Your Bike,** *Duke Street Hill; tel. 378-6669.* Also try **Savilles Cycle Store,** *97-99 Battersea Rise; tel. 228-4279,* or **Stuart Bikes,** *309 Horn Lane; tel. 993-3484.*

Chapter II

London is not a city that grabs you by the stomach like Paris or Rome; it is not a city that lights a fire under your feet like Cairo or Hong Kong. Yet to walk down its gilded streets with money in your pocket—preferably a lot of money—is to feel something remarkable, to feel quite simply at the heart of something fine, something finer maybe than anything else in the world, even if that something is not what it was once. For London is an imperial city, the capital of an empire—even if the empire no longer exists—with all the deckings, finery, and grace you'd expect. A heart beats here, not as strongly as before, but listen and you'll hear it. It's in the cries of the newsie, the patois of the tailor, the all-knowing chuckle of the publican. It's even in the names of the buildings: Canada House, South Africa House.

London's power came primarily from its rule of the sea. Once upon a time, the city's sea power was something to behold—even if it was hidden behind so many layers of luxury. Gentlemen certainly didn't reek of the docks. They might enjoy a glass of port or rum or a smoke from some far distant land, and a few, such as Sherlock Holmes and Wilde's Dorian Grey, might steal down to the docks at night to visit the opium dens run by Chinese. But salt air, by and large, was for impressed gangs of sailors.

Today, London's sea power truly has vanished—but its heritage has not. And the place to marvel at this heritage—even more than the stately buildings along Regent Street or the great facades of Piccadilly—is the **British Museum,** *Great Russell Street; tel. 636-1555,* which brims with the loot of conquest—with more mummies than you'll find in Egypt, with perhaps the finest sculptures produced in ancient Greece, with magnificent pottery from Islam, and with the cream of Chinese porcelain. All the loot those noble British ships brought back.

Ms. Wilde was folding up her umbrella as we passed through a group of chic French schoolgirls taking one anothers' photographs as though posing for *Vogue*.

"Quite a remarkable umbrella," I said.

"Yes. My groups can always find me." I imagine they can, I thought to myself. Ms. Wilde was an extremely attractive woman. I felt rather flattered to be her only guest.

"A Briggs umbrella," I said.

"Why, you have a good eye."

We seemed to be hitting it off. I don't know that I'd call myself a rake, but I was damned attracted to this woman within five minutes of seeing her. She walked me into the museum and through the bookstore, oddly enough the way to the chief museum treasures, almost as though we were making our way through a maze. She nodded to an Arabic-looking gentleman standing before the counter selling replicas of Egyptian artifacts. A moment later, we were standing in front of a chiseled stone that looked either like a marble plaque in a park or something that had fallen from outer space. It bore three incredibly small but distinct patches of writing. The Rosetta Stone.

It's no easy matter to discern the meaning of something old. Ms. Wilde explained to me how the French scholar Champollion pieced together what every priest had once known, the meaning of Egyptian hieroglyphics and the more popular demotic script. It is amazing how much we have recovered; we have no way of

The British Museum.

24

knowing what we have lost. I thought of how residents of Rome actually forgot where the Forum was. And how Christianity all but died out in the seventh century, except for a few priests in Ireland.

The copy of *Beowulf* in the museum's prints and drawing collection is the only one that remains. It made me wonder what may have escaped us. As I was pondering these thoughts, Ms. Wilde began to explain how the Rosetta Stone and the other priceless treasures I was seeing came to England after Nelson defeated Napoleon on the Nile in 1802, two colonizers arguing over spoils. She became quite passionate on the subject.

"England stole this from France, who stole it from Egypt. We have more Egyptian artifacts here than you'll find in the Egyptian Museum. Or do you doubt that, Mr. Woods?"

"I didn't say I doubted it." Her tone was oddly aggressive. "I spent some time in Egypt," I ventured. "But anyway, isn't it better the things are safe? In Cairo, you still can bribe the guards to sell you a keepsake. I did it," I explained.

She turned away. As though to prove her point, she marched me to the Duveen Gallery and the Elgin Marbles from the frieze of the Parthenon, carved under the direction of Athens' greatest sculptor, Phidias. During the long period of Ottoman rule of Greece, in 1810, Lord Elgin, then ambassador to Constantinpole, obtained the marbles from the sultan and sold them to the museum for £35,000. Ms. Wilde explained how Greece has tried—unsuccessfully—to get them back.

"They never will," she said. "The English are too acquisitive."

I raised my eyebrows. We went upstairs to look at the mummies. Ms. Wilde pointed out a well-preserved specimen, No. 22542, bearing the caption, "From the coffin of an unknown princess from Thebes, 21st dynasty." As I stared at this unfortunate shrink-wrapped princess, whose remains now make popular viewing, Ms. Wilde explained that the mummy was cursed.

An obscure Egyptian mummy about 3,500 years old.

25

"The bloke who discovered this mummy dropped dead on the spot," she said with untidy relish. "Indeed, Mr. Woods, it's a wonder you can see it at all." She paused. "This mummy was part of the cargo of the *Titanic*."

"What are we doing here?" I asked. At that three schoolchildren ran up, put there hands on the edge of the case, looked in, made faces, and ran off to do the same before a cat.

"No less an authority than Sir E. A. Wallis-Budge, the curator of Egyptian antiquities, was convinced that this mummy was cursed." Ms. Wilde went on. "And that curse befalls all who behold it."

"You really know how to take care of your clients," I said.

"All these mummies were the bodies of kings and queens, considered gods, destined for the next world, Mr. Woods. They were buried with accouterments for the next life and protected by magic curses." Around us, the bright fluorescent room was positively humid from the guidebook- and camera-laden crowds.

"Do you suppose this is the afterlife?" I asked.

She laughed. "I wonder what the royal family would say if their tombs were dug up and their bodies displayed for gawking tourists. Known only as numbers. For take away the numbers, and it is difficult to tell one mummy from another, one queen's hand mirror from that of another."

As she said that, her hand went to her neck.

"Indeed, you are wearing an Egyptian-looking necklace, aren't you?" I said. She was, of small turquoise beads.

"But you are observant. I buy these from a friend, the same who supplies the museum shop. You know, just a bit of buffing, and this would seem old. In fact, Mr. Woods, are you sure your momentos from Egypt are real—not just something for the tourists?" She laughed. "If I were you, I might hope they were the latter." Her stare seemed rather intense.

"Better the mummies had never left their tomb," I murmured. "Better modern man had never discovered it, better England should never have ventured from her shores." I looked up for her reaction. She was smiling. "Better we had never come here," I continued.

"And that the curse had never fallen where it will," she added.

"Shall we move on?" I asked. We progressed through various civilizations: Assyrian, Cretan, Babylonian, Trojan, even European. At last we were all the way around the building in the pleasantly dusty documents room. Here, locked up in cases, we passed ancient Bibles, a manuscript of *Lord Jim* by Conrad, a manuscript of *Jane Eyre* by Bronte, and the Magna Carta. Enough to make a hack like me feel humble, but a vast improvement over the mummies. Ms. Wilde spoke a few words with a guard, and we entered the reading room of the library. Not much to see; the scholars looked as sober as ever. Who would imagine that one of them, like Marx, might change history?

After the reading room, we left the museum and crossed the street to have a beer at the Museum Tavern. This tranquil pub (where Marx drank) held more scholars than tourists.

After a pint, we walked by the house of **Virginia Woolf,** *51 Gordon Square,* where Woolf once entertained the Bloomsbury Group. From there to the **Courtauld Institute Galleries,** where we took a brief walk through European art history from the Renaissance to the 19th century—the collection is small but superbly rich in works by impressionists, including Cézanne, Gaugin, Renoir, Van Gogh, and Manet. The collection features Van Gogh's *Self Portrait with Bandaged Ear* and Manet's *Bar at the Folies Bergère,* along with works by local Bloomsbury painters, notably Roger Fry. (This collection will move to Somerset House on the Strand by 1989.)

While in this quiet, green neighborhood, you should not miss **Dickens' house,** *48 Doughty St.; tel. 405-2127,* where, from 1837 through 1839, the author wrote parts of the *Pickwick Papers* and *Oliver Twist.* If you've any love of literature, you'll enjoy looking at the manuscripts here. The house is open to the public Monday through Saturday from 10 a.m. to 5 p.m. Admission is £1.50.

This Chinese beaker from the Wan Li period (1573-1619) is displayed at the British Museum.

Bloomsbury is also home of the **Percival-Davis Foundation of Chinese Art,** *53 Gordon Square,* which houses a fantastic collection of pottery; **Pollock's Toy Museum and Shop,** *1 Scala St.; tel. 636-3452* (open Monday through Saturday from 10 a.m. to 5 p.m.; admission is 60p, 30p for children); and **London University,** founded in 1827 by Utilitarian Jeremy Bentham as an alternative to Anglican Oxford and Cambridge. Nondenominational and on the Continental model, London University admitted Jews and Catholics.

Not far from Bloomsbury, in Holborn, is the **John Soane Museum,** *13 Lincoln's Inn Fields,* the house of the eccentric architect.

But for me, these sights would have to wait for another day. By the time we left the Courtauld Gallery, I was more than a little tired. The charming Ms. Woods, moreover, had an appointment. We stood at the corner of Bloomsbury Square. To the west, the fall sky was beginning to deepen and bruise. She smiled at me in a way that I couldn't forget that night—indeed not until I saw her again.

This 17th-century English rocking horse is housed at the Victoria and Albert Museum.

"Mr. Woods, I do hope I'll see you again. You are an intelligent American. And I want to help you with your book. But now I must run."

Behind her I saw a car pull up. It was a royal green Jaguar. On the right side, a dark-haired man rolled down the window. He wore sunglasses, and his hair was slicked back with oil. Ms. Wilde glanced back, then turned, tossing the brollie back over her shoulder.

28

"'Til next time," she said. "Call me."

"I will," I answered.

She turned smartly and hurried over to the car. It seemed entirely strange that she could have planned our trip to have a car pick her up. I watched the car speed away, then paused for a moment to stare at the inky sky beyond the British Museum, veined red and pink. I felt melancholia, but then a great wave of wonder. A foreign city, money in my pocket, and in the background the amazing and stirring Ms. Wilde.

* * *

But what I should do now is to tell you something about accommodations in London. After all, my purpose is to write a guidebook about London, not a romance novel.

Accommodations

Bed and breakfasts

What in the countryside is a marvelous English institution, in London proper suffers from the high cost of space. London bed and breakfasts (B&Bs) are, as a rule, disheartening. Virtually all offer small rooms at unattractive prices. A few, however, partially make up for these problems with strong measures of charm. Generally, though, London is a place where you must spend quite a lot of money at a luxury hotel to live in a civilized manner.

Stay on the first floor (the second floor in American parlance) if possible. Most B&Bs were once townhouses, and the ceilings and windows shrink as you move upward to former children's and servants' quarters.

Bed and breakfasts do start you off well with a good English breakfast, usually of orange juice, eggs with ham, sausage, or lean Irish bacon, toast with marmalade and butter, and coffee or tea. It is rare to be served kippers (a Scottish specialty) at a London B&B, but you may be offered some tomatoes and mushrooms as garnish to your meal. The high price of space forces many B&Bs to serve breakfast in the basement, although a few have set aside ground-floor rooms for this purpose.

Hotels

Discretion and service are the hallmarks of British hotels. The best feature servants rather than employees, who seem to genuinely care for and cater to the guests. Newer hotels offer better facilities—saunas and secretaries—but often lack that something English. You may have to choose between a more private, more established hotel and a more public, better equipped one. Members of the nobility stay at the older hotels, particularly Claridge's; businessmen favor the newer places. Alas, even some of the new luxury hotels have small rooms.

Following is a list of hotels in London that I can recommend. They are arranged according to underground stops.

Claridge's, a luxury hotel favored by the nobility.

Bayswater and Nottinghill Gate

• **Portobello Hotel,** *22 Stanley Gardens, W1; tel. 727-2777; tube: Nottinghill Gate. £92 for a double room, including breakfast.*

People either love the Portobello or hate it. Within walking distance of Portobello Road, the hotel attracts visiting antiques dealers. A laissez-faire spirit prevails. The restaurant stays open 24 hours a day. Some suites are grand, other rooms are known as cabins. Competitively priced, the Portobello has a charm all its own. (But don't blame me if you hate it.)

Bloomsbury and Holborn

• **Berners,** *Berners Street, W1; tel. 636-1629; tube: Tottenham Court Road. £118 for a double room.*

Well situated near Bloomsbury and wonderfully well appointed, Berners combines grace and space. Twelve rooms have been specifically outfitted for the handicapped. Outer rooms can be noisy.

• **Inverness Court,** *1 Inverness Terrace, W2; tel. 229-1444; tube: Queensway. £57 for a double room.*

Built for Lily Langtry by Edward VII (to woo this lady, he also had Rules, the restaurant, remodeled), this hotel stands out from countless others in the neighborhood. For a truly royal experience, rent the Langtry Suite, which comes with a four-poster bed and a decadent sunken bath.

• **Wansbeck,** *6 Bedford Place, WC1; tel. 636-6232; tube: Russell Square. £39 for a double room, including breakfast.*

The German management keeps this bed and breakfast spotlessly clean. Breakfast is served in a bright, elegant room, and carpets clash less than usual. The rooms are typically small, but every one has a television.

Covent Garden and the Strand

• **Fielding,** *4 Broad Court and Bow Street; WC2; tel. 836-8305; tube: Covent Garden. £55.20 for a double room.*

This no-frills hotel in unlikely Covent Garden nevertheless possesses a lot of character—from the parrot that greets you at the door to the opera singers and dancers from the nearby Royal Opera House who stay here. The Fielding is reasonably priced.

• **Savoy,** *the Strand, WC2; tel. 836-4343; tube: Charing Cross. £150 for a double room.*

Built on the site of a palace that was erected in the 13th century by the Count of Savoy and blown up a century later by rebels following the socialist John Ball, the Savoy has had a colorful history. D'Oyly Carte built the Savoy theater to house his Gilbert and Sullivan productions in 1881. A decade later he opened his hotel, which incorporated the latest improvements from America.

The Savoy remains a favorite among movie stars. Although the staff can be surly, and a few rooms are down-at-heel, after the Ritz, the Savoy offers the best tea in town, its grill is famed, and its riverfront restaurant is gorgeous. Insist on a room facing the river. (For the record, the Savoy's driveway is the only street in London where traffic flows on the right.)

• **Waldorf,** *Aldwych, WC2; tel. 836-2400; tube: Aldwych. £150 for a double room.*

Convenient to Covent Garden, the courts,

31

and the city, the Waldorf is a bustling first-class hotel that just misses first-tier status. Still, its ornate Edwardian decoration and standards of comfort, including minibars in the bedrooms and old-fashioned tea dances, keep it humming with activity.

Hampstead and Highgate

• **Swiss Cottage Hotel,** *4 Adamson Road, NW3; tel. 722-2281; tube: Swiss Cottage. £30 for a double room, including breakfast.*

This friendly place is half-hotel, half-bed and breakfast. It offers 24-hour room service, accepts credit cards, and runs a restaurant—but service can be erratic. Special touches include a grand piano, Tabriz rugs, a sauna, and the delightful Honeymoon Cottage in the garden. Convenient to tube stations and bus stops, the Swiss Cottage provides a good alternative to more expensive hotels downtown.

Kensington and Chelsea

• **Alexander,** *9 Sumner Place, SW7; tel. 581-1591; tube: South Kensington. £80 for a double room, including breakfast.*

Canopied, four-poster beds are one of the attractions of the Alexander, a small hotel situated in a converted Victorian townhouse in South Kensington. A self-service (honor-system) bar in the lounge adds to the general homey feeling.

• **Blakes,** *33-35 Roland Gardens, SW7; tel. 370-6701; tube: South Kensington. £155 for a double room.*

Situated a bit off the beaten track in elegant Kensington, Blakes is a favorite among rock stars, movie folk, and the like. Occupying a townhouse and painted an anomalous green with a restaurant that's totally black, Blakes reminds me of the Rolling Stones' alleged devil worship. Still, the decor is refreshing, featuring brass beds and bird cages. The food is quite good, and the downstairs bar is extremely private—almost like a club.

• **Number Sixteen,** *16 Sumner Place, SW7; tel. 589-5232; tube: South Kensington. £95 for a double room, including breakfast.*

Like the Alexander, Number Sixteen combines a good location with a homey atmosphere. An honor-system bar and breakfast in guests' rooms contribute to a sense of well-being that attracts people in the arts. The garden is particularly pleasant.

• **Vicarage Hotel,** *10 Vicarage Gate, W8; tel. 229-4030; tube: High Street Kensington. £33 for a double room, including breakfast.*

Recently renovated, the Vicarage fills a little more slowly than the **Abbey House** next door, *tel. 727-2594.* But it's clean and friendly. And when you stay at the Vicarage, you're a neighbor to Charles and Di.

Knightsbridge and Belgravia

• **Basil Street Hotel,** *8 Basil St., SW3; tel. 581-33111; tube: Knightsbridge. £101 for a double room.*

Once a woman's hotel reserved for ladies shopping in Knightsbridge, the Basil Street retains a feminine touch—although men are now welcome. Antiques, a cozy Edwardian building, and good service make it a favorite small hotel.

• **Capital Hotel,** *22-24 Basil Street, SW3; tel. 589-5171; tube: Knightsbridge. £150 for a double room.*

Renowned for its informal luxury, the Capital Hotel excels in the personal touch. Bathrobes are supplied for guests, and freshly cut roses are given to ladies staying here. Interconnecting rooms are convenient for families or groups. The Capital has a good French restaurant.

• **Hyde Park,** *Knightsbridge, SW1; tel. 235-2000; tube: Knightsbridge. £170 for a double room.*

Prominently defending Hyde Park corner, with many rooms facing the park, the Hyde Park Hotel is a London fixture. Brunch facing the park is particularly pleasant.

• **Wilbraham Hotel,** *1 Wilbraham Place, SW1; tel. 730-8296; tube: Sloane Square. £53 for a double room.*

Brown's.

The Wilbraham Hotel offers one of the best values in London. Situated in elegant—if slightly sterile—Belgravia, it retains the staircases, archways, and other Victorian details of the townhouses it inhabits. Porters carry your bags, you can have breakfast served in your room, and the staff turns down the beds at night. Credit cards are not accepted.

Marylebone

• **Durrants,** George Street, W1; tel. 935-8131; tube: Bond Street. £80 for a double room.

Durrants is known for its beauty, good service, and value, all within sight of the Wallace Collection. Special touches include an open fire in the bar, a writing room, and brass beds in many rooms. Durrants is one of the best values in London.

Mayfair and St. James's

• **Athenaeum,** 116 Piccadilly, W1; tel. 499-3463 or (800)223-5560 from the United States; tube: Green Park. £155 for a double room.

One of London's small but fine hotels, the Athenaeum excels in detail. Whatever your needs, the staff will satisfy them. Neither cheap nor grand, it is nonetheless elegant.

• **Brown's,** 22-24 Dover St., W1; tel. 493-6020; tube: Green Park. £165 for a double room.

Founded by Lord Byron's butler and now owned by Trusthouse Forte, Brown's has developed a rich, gentlemanly languor over the centuries. A private hotel (but still more open than the Connaught), it features good food and charm. However, some of the rooms are small. Like all of London's fine hotels, Brown's has its quotient of famous devotees, particularly writers.

• **Claridge's,** Brook Street, W1; tel. 629-8860; tube: Bond Street. £185 for a double room.

Claridge's has an aristocratic gilt. During World War II, it was home to the king of Greece and the king of Luxembourg, and it has been a favorite among royalty since the 19th century. The lift features a luxurious couch. The hotel has no bar but two good eateries: the gastronomic Restaurant and the informal Causerie, known for its luncheon smorgasbord.

34

This is the kind of place that remembers your favorite room and sees to it that the same staff members attend you each time you return.

• **Connaught,** *16 Carlos Place, W1; tel. 499-7070; tube: Bond Street. £158 for a double room.*

Considered by devotees the finest hotel in the world, the Connaught is relatively inexpensive, luxuriously private, and booked up weeks, sometimes months in advance. The hotel works to make guests feel they're staying in the home of a trusted friend. To this end, no shops or services are permitted to litter the lobby. To pass though the gate of the Connaught is to enter a preserve of bygone graciousness. Most rooms have open fires.

Renowned for its Grill Room, the hotel also has a one-star (from Michelin) restaurant and a paneled bar (where Tony mixes them). The hotel is in a particularly pleasant part of Mayfair—a few steps from St. George's Gardens. MasterCard, but not American Express, is accepted.

• **Dukes Hotel,** *33-36 St. James's Place, SW1; tel. 491-4840; tube: Green Park. £170 for a double room.*

A small, exclusive hotel in St. James's, Dukes has much in common with neighborhood clubs, such as Brooks and Boodles. Fortunately, standards of food and comfort are higher. Dukes Hotel, which occupies a townhouse in a charming gas-lit courtyard, offers an oasis of calm, only minutes from the bustle of Piccadilly and just around the corner from Christies.

• **Grosvenor House,** *Park Lane, W1; tel. 499-6363; tube: Marble Arch. £185 for a double room.*

Facing Hyde Park, Grosvenor House features the fine Pavilion Restaurant and the Lounge, where you can enjoy traditional afternoon tea. The top floor is home to the Crown Club—an exclusive room open only to club members (usually businesspeople).

• **Inn on the Park,** *Hamilton Place, Park Lane, W1; tel. 499-0888; tube: Hyde Park Corner. £184 for a double room.*

Inn on the Park offers the luxury and exceptional service you'd expect at these prices. It's located in a 1950s building that has been decorated with well-chosen antiques.

• **Meridien Piccadilly,** *Piccadilly, W1; tel. 734-8000; tube: Green Park. £165 for a double room.*

Unlike most London hotels, which grew by devouring adjoining townhouses, the Piccadilly was built as a whole in 1908. Complete with swimming pools and Turkish baths, it was the most advanced hotel of its day. However, after its glory days during the 1920s, the hotel went into decline. It was refurbished in the early 1980s by the French firm Meridien. Now it has the best facilities, business and health, of any hotel in London. One of its restaurants, the Oak Room, was recently awarded a Michelin star. The hotel's pleasant rooms and suites, each decorated differently, offer all the luxury you could want in the style of all the grand hotels of the Continent. Did you see the movie with Garbo?

• **Park Lane,** *Piccadilly, W1; tel. 499-6321; tube: Hyde Park Corner. £159.95 for a double room.*

The Park Lane is not on Park Lane, but down the street on Piccadilly—an inconsistency that perfectly captures the quirkiness of this hotel. A well-appointed luxury hotel, the Park Lane offers fine examples of art-deco decor, particularly in its restaurant.

• **Ritz,** *Piccadilly, W1; tel. 493-8181; tube: Green Park. £175 for a double room.*

César Ritz founded his first great hotel in Paris, but then took his talent to London. While running the London Ritz, rival hotelier and Gilbert and Sullivan producer D'Oyly Carte used characteristic guile to hire Ritz away to run the Savoy— and to make its reputation. If possible, insist on a room facing Green Park. Now owned by Cunard, the Ritz is an open hotel, and its Palm Court is the place for Sunday tea. Non-residents must book in advance.

• **Stafford Hotel,** *16-18 St. James's Place, SW1; tel. 493-0111; tube: Green Park. £155 for a double room.*

The Meridien Piccadilly.

The elegant Stafford in stately St. James's inherited the wine cellars of the palace. The hotel keeps them well stocked—and well-heeled patrons keep them active. The friendly management and tranquil location have made this hotel popular among travelers. Many consider it a better deal than its Park Lane competitors.

• **Westbury,** *Conduit Street, W1; tel. 629-7755; tube: Bond Street. £165 for a double room.*

The New York Westbury, a polo ground on Long Island, inspired the London hotel of the same name in 1955. Owned by Trusthouse Forte, the London Westbury, with its Polo bar and open fire in the sitting room, retains the spirit of 1950s America, lacking only Steve Allen on the television.

Victoria Station and Pimlico

• **Ebury Court,** *26 Ebury St., SW1; tel. 730-8147; tube: Victoria Station or Sloane Square. £72 for a double room, including breakfast.*

From the balconies of rooms facing the front, you can watch the guards march to Buckingham Palace. English breakfast includes smoked haddock and kippers; dinner is served as well. (To drink in the hotel's bar, you must join a club.) More a place for families than singles, the Ebury Court makes up in welcome what it lacks in space.

• **Goring Hotel,** *15 Beeston Place, SW1; tel. 834-8211; tube: Victoria Station. £130 for a double room.*

George Goring, the proprietor of this pleasant hotel, is a hotelier of the old school. (His grandfather installed the first central heating system and universal baths in London.) This full-service hotel remains in family hands, and Goring will see that it continues to remain so. The Goring is perhaps your best chance to visit a truly traditional English hotel.

Chapter III

London is a great city for long, rambling walks. Different hours of the day reveal different sides of its character. And the different neighborhoods reflect its village composition, for London is made up of many villages. Bloomsbury is close enough to the city so that in the evening the streets (and pubs) are filled with financial workers in suits, having a few before going home.

After a short nap at my hotel, I headed out for a walk before dinner. I wandered vaguely south in the direction of Soho. Drinkers in suits and skinheads in undershirts spilled out onto the street in front of the pub on Shaftesbury, next to the Café Bordeaux, which is a good if bright French restaurant (the veal filets are delicious).

Crossing the street my eye was caught by the mimeographed hand-scrawled poster for the *Evening Standard*. "MI5 shoot out at Charing Cross." I bought the paper and began to devour the story. "At Charing Cross shots were exchanged today between officials believed to be from MI5 and several men. The government would not comment on the affair. Nor did a check of nearby hospital casualty wards turn up any persons admitted. But witnesses told of a confrontation between officials who stopped traffic and Arabic-speaking fugitives."

It seemed incredible that I had seen this very drama. I threw the paper away. I have a healthy disrespect for the *Standard*—and the rest of Britain's tabloids.

As night began to fall, I made my way to Covent Garden, down Neal Street. The boutiques along here were closed, but their brightly lit windows displayed gorgeous sweaters and jackets. I saw that the Neal Street Restaurant was still going strong, as was the fringe theater here, the Donmar Warehouse. It is always more fun to dine with a friend, so at the first payphone I took out my address book and dialed a few numbers. I was surprised to hear answering machines in old England. Technology is everywhere.

I finally tried my old friend Jim MacAllister, a Scotsman who covers London for a Glasgow paper. He picked up on the second ring.

"Well imagine that, in London. Yeh must come over at woonce." But when I told him where I was, he decided to come out instead. He told me to meet him at the Café des Amis du Vin, a half-step up from the Opera House on tiny Hanover Place. If I knew my impecunious friend, the food would be superb but not too expensive.

The Café des Amis du Vin says it all in its name. Are we not all friends of wine? A wine bar in the basement provides the genial, romantic foundation for this three-tier restaurant, recently acquired (but respected) by Trusthouse Forte. A brasserie on the ground floor rings with good cheer, but Jim took me upstairs to the quieter dining room (which is priced about the same). The service was friendly and precise.

The English are masters of quaint little dining rooms.

London restaurants have a strange habit of stinting on bread. Even many of the best restaurants bring you a silver tray laden with tasteless rolls and allow you to pick just one. Occasionally I've managed to get two before the waiter aggressively yanked the tray away, but it's never easy. However, at the Café des Amis du Vin, a plate of good French bread arrived—as it should.

We began talking at once about the good old days. We'd been in Egypt together, Jim with the BBC. I ordered snails with a cognac and cream sauce in puff pastry followed by a filet of veal in a green pepper mousse. Jim announced himself partial to the smoked salmon with crab mousse, followed by poached seafood flavored with saffron. We washed it down with lots of the good house wine, then finished with a superb assortment of cheeses.

I mentioned the story of shots at Charing Cross. Jim doubted I'd see more (the Official Secrets Act allows the government to put a lid on such matters). He treated me to a short lecture on the differences between the English and American systems.

"We don't have a bill of rights. The government can pass any law it likes. Take these new bills, for example."

He explained the raging debate over the government's new law that says citizens no longer have the right to remain silent. Silence now counts against you. What's more, journalists may no longer report views in the paper that are sympathetic in the least to terrorists—no matter who expresses them. Jim further explained that the party in power introduces all new legislation. The opposition can sponsor bills only one day a year. Clearly, a parliamentary system gives the party in power more power than in the United States.

"London's changing, that's all. You know how it is, John. A whole new world. No more Fleet Street. We all work in Wapping now in high-security compounds. So we do our drinking in the canteen." He was referring to the move of the papers from Fleet

The West India Docks.

41

Street to non-union facilities in the Docklands, perhaps the biggest development in Europe recently.

I insisted on buying Jim a drink. He chose a single malt scotch; I had a tawny port. After settling the comparatively reasonable bill of about £50, we stumbled out into sparkling Covent Garden.

Like many old European markets, Covent Garden hit a low a few years back, overrun with rats and unsuited to modern lorries. Developed by Inigo Jones, an Elizabethan set designer turned architect for Charles I, Covent Garden blossomed in the 18th century following the Puritan closing of theaters and pubs south of the river (where Shakespeare had plied his trade). The first theater charter was granted in 1660, and for two centuries thereafter the area became the stomping ground of Goldsmith, Hogarth, Fielding, and assorted Libertine noblemen.

With the creation of Shaftesbury Avenue in 1887 and the host of speculative construction that followed, the theater district shifted to Soho. But Covent Garden retains its associations. In 1974, the sprawling market—where Henry Higgins met Elizabeth Doolittle in *Pygmalian*—moved to Nine Elms, south of the river. And in 1980, the run-down piazza—site of the then-seedy punk club the Rock Garden—was redeveloped into the pleasant shopping mall it has become. (The Rock Garden has grown into a sidewalk café.)

Covent Garden Market in 1867.

Jim and I walked over to the Punch and Judy Pub, which houses a museum (the first Punch and Judy show was performed here in 1662), and had a drink in the crowded upstairs wine bar. He told me the basement pub is a hangout for *au pair* girls. I glanced in and judged this to be true.

From there we headed over to the equally crowded but preferable Brahms and Liszt, where fashionable media people were drinking not glasses but bottles of wine—the thing to do in a wine bar.

But Covent Garden has more to offer than wine bars. Pretty **St. Paul's Cathedral** at the west end is all that survives of Inigo Jones' creation (it was rebuilt after the war). It has long associations with the theater. Walk around back and look at the tender in-

St. Paul's Cathedral.

scriptions on the gravestones of numerous thespians, who now lie where in life they played. "I have come in to my garden," reads one.

The **Cabaret Mechanical Theatre,** *33-34 the Market* (the entrance is by the Punch and Judy Pub), is worth seeing (wooden puppets act out skits at the push of a button). At the southeast corner of Covent Garden is the **Transport Museum,** which lovers of trains will appreciate. Most interesting to me is the **Theatre Museum,** *Russell Street,* with its treasure of sets, costumes, and other memorabilia from an art that is otherwise so marvelously transient.

I grew tired of standing at the Brahms and Liszt. I guess Jim did, too, because he suggested we leave Covent Garden, a fine but trendy place, and finish the evening at the Savoy, at the comfortable American Bar, not particularly crowded at that hour. From there, Jim was all for going on to Annabel's, the disco. It wasn't often, he explained, that he got to see such an old friend. Why not do the town? But, truth be told, I was too far in my port. We stumbled into our respective cabs, and I rolled down the window to let the night air stream in. I was glad to have seen my old friend, glad to be alive and in London, gladder still to be going to bed.

At the desk, the concierge handed me a message. I read it in the yellow light of the lift. "Please call as soon as possible—Jenny Wilde." But it was all I could do to get out of my clothes and into some old pajamas. I tumbled onto my incredibly comfortable bed and began dreaming about the raging sands of the Sinai.

* * *

Time, again, I suppose, to don my tour guide's hat and offer some restaurant recommendations.

Dining out

It's not always easy to find good food in London. It exists, but you've got to know where to look. Although London's best restaurants compare favorably with any in the world, good cooking is not a national vocation, nor is good food considered the natural right of the citizenry, as in France and Italy. It is a privilege, and you must approach it as such. So plan in advance—and make reservations.

However, even if you don't eat as well here as in other cities, you will do so in pleasant surroundings. The English are masters of quaint little dining rooms.

If England offers one great value in food, it is smoked fish. I advise gobbling up all the smoked Scottish salmon, kippers, and smoked mackerel you can get your hands on. When you get home, you'll be glad you did.

If you're looking for a hot meal at an odd hour, try an Indian restaurant. Indeed, if Michelin were an Indian company instead of a French one, London would have more than its paltry 19 stars. London's Indian restaurants have a virtual lock on the late-night, after-the-pubs-close market and play a major role in London courtship.

The *tandoori* dishes that you'll see on every Indian restaurant's menu consist of lean meats marinated in a sauce of spices and yogurt and barbecued in a very dry clay oven. A truly wonderful flavor. The traditional red color comes from food dye. (In India, the famous *tandoori* is recognized by its color.) *Tandoori* (or *tikka*) *masala* is particularly good. It consists of *tandoori* meat served in a delicious creamy sauce. *Curry masala* is a traditional *curry* made with tomatoes and onion. *Vindaloo* is hotter. *Bhuna* is made with cream. *Biriani* is a main dish of rice, raisins, and chopped nuts. Indian breads are good, especially *poori* (layered and puffy) and *nan* (cooked in the *tandoori* oven).

The city's pubs are good places to have a hot meal at lunchtime. Generally, I counsel avoiding sandwich shops.

Popular pub dishes include the ploughman's lunch (usually cheese, bread, and pickles), bubble and squeak (named for how it sounds cooking, this dish consists of recooked cabbage and potatoes), quiche, and bangers (sausages). Jellied eel is a cockney specialty. Stilton, a piquant variation of Roquefort, stands out among popular cheeses. Favorite desserts include treacle roll (treacle is like jam) and bread pudding.

Your best bet is to eat only at mealtimes. London has few places to have a snack. You may be able to find an edible vegetable samosa, but England does not excel in this category. If you get hungry between meals, look for a croissant shop or grab some fish and chips.

The hallmark of British cuisine is the joint. Joints are large roasts, often carved in front of you. Grills (of fish, beef, or lamb) follow a close second. If you're in the mood for fish, try the Dover sole, some of the best fish in the world. English oysters are good and good for you, and Dublin prawns hold court in the world of shrimp.

English cuisine in general emphasizes meat and fish. Most dishes, even in the best restaurants, are served not with sauces but gravy. Local specialties include beef and kidney or beef and oyster pie, shepherds pie (which consists of ground meat baked with mashed potatoes), cottage pie (which is shepherds pie *sans* onion), and bangers and mash (sausages with potatoes).

The Savoy has long been an experience in elegant dining.

London has many Italian restaurants, but none are particularly spectacular. It's as though these hot-blooded southerners, deprived of their native sun, have lost touch with their senses. (However, that does not mean you won't find tasty pasta at the Italian restaurants listed below.)

Restaurants

The following list of restaurants is organized according to underground stops.

Bayswater and Nottinghill Gate

• **Khan's,** *13-15 Westbourne Grove, W2; tel. 727-5420.*

People always seem to be having a good time at Khan's. This is not the place for an intimate tête à tête, but Khan's makes up in sheer, noisy extravagance what it lacks in intimacy. If possible, choose a table in the high-ceilinged front room, where you can dine among artificial palms and admire the painted walls. Weekends you must take your place in the queue.

Camden Town and Islington

• **Nontas,** *16 Camden High St., NW1; tel. 387-4579; tube: Camden Town.*

Camden Town has a large Greek-Cypriot population, a result of hostilities on that island. The fortunate fruit for the diner are the many reasonably priced Greek restaurants here. Nontas, easy to find on Camden High Street and downright cheap by London standards, offers particularly good fare, notably the *mezze*.

The City

• **George & Vulture,** *3 Castle Court, EC3; tel. 626-9710.*

Down a narrow alley adjacent to St. Michael's Church, the George & Vulture serves authentic British cooking. Not the place for a leisurely meal, rather this is the place to experience British camaraderie at its bulliest. The (male) stockbrokers at the tables might well be sailors at mess, schoolboys in their dining hall, even Beowulf's pals in the mead hall. Whoever they are, they're having fun. Try the chops or one of the other grills, and wash your meal down with ale.

• **Sweetings,** *39 Queen Victoria St., EC4; tel. 248-3062; tube: Mansion House.*

One of the oldest seafood restaurants in London, Sweetings is also one of the best. Reservations aren't required. Make your way to the back of the restaurant and take a seat at one of the communal tables, or create a space for yourself at the bar. Don't expect sauces, just good fish as fresh as it comes. Only lunch is served.

Covent Garden and the Strand

• **Boulestin,** *1a Henrietta St. (on the piazza), WC2; tel. 836-7061.*

Downstairs from Covent Garden, Boulestin is a London tradition. Although the restaurant is entirely underground, when you are dining here, you feel you are in a country house, an effect achieved by original oils depicting horses, rich wallpaper, and dark autumnal hues. Service is impeccable, and the cuisine is good (but less than *haute*). You can do much worse. Save room for the delicious desserts, which include a chocolate demitasse filled with a white chocolate mousse. Also sample the 1900 Castarede Armagnac (£40 per glass).

• **Café des Amis du Vin,** *11-14 Hanover Place, WC2; tel. 379-3444.*

Just a few steps from the Opera House, Café des Amis du Vin is a Covent Garden secret. Not that the place isn't crowded—but it escapes the run of tourists. A warm, inviting wine bar in the basement gives way to a spirited brasserie on the first floor and a quiet, elegant, and excellent restaurant upstairs. Prices are reasonable, and the service is gracious and friendly. Do not miss the cheese board.

• **Café du Jardin,** *28 Wellington St., WC2; tel. 836-8769.*

In England, enjoying a good French meal more often than not requires making reservations in advance and dressing up for the occasion—in other words, a lot of trouble. As a result, the Café du Jardin is a welcome institution, where you can drop in for decent French cooking at

The Savoy of 1650 decorates the cover of the menu for the Grill Room.

prices that promote *liberté*. Simple dishes include steak with a *confit* of onions and chicken with champagne sauce. A cheap pre-theater menu is available, and the house wine is both drinkable and reasonably priced.

- **Calabash,** *38 King St., WC2; tel. 836-1976.*

Probably London's best African restaurant, Calabash excels in spicy, exotic dishes from West Africa, both French and English. Ensconced within the scholarly African Centre, the atmosphere reeks of Oxbridge. Try chicken in coconut milk or beef stew with pine nuts and spinach, and wash it all down with Tusker beer. (The African Centre also sponsors interesting exhibitions.)

- **Food for Thought,** *31 Neal St., WC2; tel. 836-0239.*

If you happen to walk down Neal Street one day at lunchtime, you may notice a long queue. The people in line know that Food for Thought sells excellent vegetarian fare to take out—or to enjoy downstairs during less crowded times—at prices that can't be beat. Much better than Cranks, although it lacks the dining facilities.

- **Grill Room** and **Restaurant,** *the Savoy, the Strand, WC2; tel. 836-4343; tube: Charing Cross.*

The famous Grill Room offers good English cooking, including daily specials and, appropriately enough, grills. Patrons come for the sake of nostalgia (Escoffier once ran the kitchen) more than they do for the food.

Oddly enough, the Grill Room, which overlooks the driveway, has always overshadowed the Savoy Restaurant, which boasts a stunning view over the Thames. I frankly prefer the latter. Its *dîner au choix* (£24.50) and *dîner aux gourmets* (£32.75) offer good English dishes (with French names) in one of the most pleasant dining rooms in England.

• **Inigo Jones,** *14 Garrick St., WC2; tel. 836-6456.*

A few steps off Garrick Street, Inigo Jones serves some of the best—if most expensive—food in this neighborhood. Situated in a former stained-glass factory, the restaurant displays souvenirs and has lots of room. The menu, which includes both bourgeois and *nouvelle-cuisine* dishes, changes frequently. The lunch and pre-dinner *prix-fixe* menu is a good way to cut costs.

• **Interlude de Tabaillau,** *7-8 Bow St., WC2; tel. 379-6473.*

Across the street from the Opera House, Interlude de Tabaillau could not be more convenient. A relatively new restaurant, however, the food does not always match the prices (even though it comes from Le Gavroche veteran Jean-Louis Taillebaud). Good *nouvelle-cuisine* dishes include an excellent *confit de quail.* Gravies, rather than sauces, provide the English accent. The *prix-fixe* menu (£24.50) comes complete with petites fours for dessert. A good place to get a table when other restaurants are booked—at least until Michelin gives it a star.

• **Rules,** *35 Maiden Lane, WC2; tel. 836-5314.*

Edward VII wooed Lilly Langtry at Rules in a specially constructed room upstairs (that allowed them to come and go unseen). Today much wooing continues—of the business variety at lunch and the more traditional variety at dinner. The homey decor has been assembled over centuries, for Rules is the oldest restaurant in England. An open fire adds to the ambience in winter.

• **Simpson's-in-the-Strand,** *100 the Strand, WC2; tel. 836-9112; tube: Covent Garden.*

Simpson's is a London institution, loved by some, disliked by others. To enter this venerable establishment is to enter what might well be a racquet club. The atmosphere is comfortable, masculine, entirely reminiscent of a boarding school. Trophies and momentos abound amid dark ancient paneling. Dining here reminds me of attending parents' day at school, the day they serve the good food on silver platters to fool the ones who are paying. The menu includes juicy joints, carved at the table, and duck in apple sauce. At £13, the pre-theater (6 p.m. to 7 p.m.) and Saturday lunch menu of smoked Scottish salmon paté, rib of beef, Yorkshire pudding, treacle roll, and coffee is a deal.

The East End

- **Blooms,** *90 Whitechapel High St., E1; tel. 247-6001.*

After World War II, many poor Jews settled in the East End to begin a climb to affluence—just as poor Jews settled in New York to begin their climb from the Lower East Side. Blooms is a legacy of that period and has become a London institution. On Sunday, a stone's throw from Petticoat Lane, it is especially crowded. Join the line. Good food includes salt (corned) beef, matzo balls, chicken soup, and borscht. The atmosphere is as real as it gets.

Hampstead and Highgate

- **Villa Bianca,** *1 Perrin's Court, NW3; tel. 435-3131.*

On pretty Perrin's Court, Villa Bianca serves good Italian food in a pleasant setting. Try the pasta or one of the other classic Italian dishes.

Kensington and Chelsea

- **Bibendum,** *81 Fulham Road, SW3; tel. 581-5817.*

Simon Hopkinson's new restaurant in the former Michelin Building, restored by Terence Conran, is named for the Michelin Man, that puffy, pneumatic playboy. Situated upstairs, it offers good food in an airy multileveled room. The service sometimes has been surly, but at the moment, the restaurant is all the rage. Make reservations in advance. Appetizers feature seafood, including cod *ceviche*; main courses include traditional roasts and grills, including steak *au poîvre*.

- **Bombay Brasserie,** *140 Courtfield Close, Coutfield Road, SW7; tel. 370-4040; tube: Gloucester Road.*

London has no shortage of good Indian restaurants, but the Bombay Brasserie may well be the best. More expensive than most, it also provides more in the way of atmosphere. Try the *tandoori* specialties or the Bombay-inspired seafood dishes.

- **Drakes,** 2a Pond Place, SW3; tel. 584-4555; tube: South Kensington.

Drakes serves good English food to businessmen at lunch and to well-heeled residents at dinner.

- **Gavvers,** 61-63 Lower Sloane St., SW1; tel. 730-5983; tube: Sloane Square.

A bit of the Roux brothers' (Michel and Albert, who hail from Charolles in Burgundy) magic, Gavvers is a younger brother to Le Gavroche. Prices are lower, the crowd younger, and the food good, if not equally *haute.* Only one menu is served, which makes Gavvers a true *prix-fixe* restaurant. Gavvers is not open for lunch.

- **Joe's Café,** 126 Draycott Ave., SW3; tel. 225-2217.

Joe's is the closest thing in London to a New York restaurant. It stays open from morning to midnight, a godsend in London to those with unusual schedules, and provides good food in a beautifully designed, yet informal setting. People dress up here because they like to, not because they feel any obligation to the management. Good if not spectacular food includes ravioli stuffed with wild mushrooms and steak *frites.* Good for weekend brunch, a bite after a performance at the Royal Court theater, or a drink after a concert at the Royal Albert Hall. Dinner is served until 11:30 p.m.

- **Ma Cuisine,** 113 Walton St., SW3; tel. 584-7585; tube: South Kensington.

For years, gourmets and gourmands alike have kept Ma Cuisine's few tables almost permanently booked. Prices are reasonable, the setting near fashionable Brompton Cross intimate, and the bistro food delicious. Try the *feuillete de saumon* or the sweetbreads stuffed with veal. Tables sometimes open up, so it's worth calling for a reservation.

- **Paper Tiger,** 10 Exhibition Road, SW7; tel. 584-3737; tube: South Kensington.

Most Chinese restaurants in London are Cantonese. For those with a taste for spice, the Paper Tiger is a welcome find, particularly in this neighborhood. Its szechuan cooking compares with the best in New York; however, prices run somewhat higher.

- **Tante Claire,** 68 Royal Hospital Road, SW3; tel. 352-6045.

In my humble opinion, this is the best restaurant in London. Many (but not Michelin) agree with me. Roux brothers alumnus M. Koffman does amazing things with fish, to wit his scallops with oysters and truffles. He also serves good ancien régime dishes, such as pigs' trotters with wild mushrooms. It was to sample the latter that Louis XVI unwisely stopped in Vincennes the night he tried to flee Paris. (The mob transported him back, mortified, but sated.) A bright, recently expanded dining room adds to the experience of communicating with the gods. The *prix-fixe* lunch (£18.50) is an excellent deal, but you must make reservations in advance.

Knightsbridge and Belgravia

• **Ménage à Trois,** *15 Beauchamp Place, SW3; tel. 584-9350; tube: Knightsbridge.*

Small *nouvelle-cuisine* portions may charm women more than men, but no one can deny that the food here is exquisite and the location on fashionable Beauchamp (pronounced Beecham) Place near Harrods convenient for mixing lunch with last night's gossip—heaven for Sloane Rangers. Order dishes according to your hunger from a selection of hors d'oeuvres and desserts. The best choices on the menu are the terrine of lobster salmon and broccoli and the peaches stuffed with pistachio ice cream.

Marylebone

• **Sea Shell,** *49 Lisson Grove, NW1; tel. 723-8703; tube: Marylebone.*

Few would disagree that the Sea Shell has the best fish and chips in town. Moist, fluffy pieces of haddock, cod, or monkfish fried in a delicate batter and served with chips from heaven will solve the food problem—as it's called in London. And for little more than tuppence.

Mayfair and St. James's

• **Hard Rock Café,** *150 Old Park Lane, W1; tel. 629-0382.*

Jimi Hendrix's guitar, loud music, and good hamburgers and shakes (even by my standards) bring young people here in droves. A good address for a hamburger joint.

• **Justin de Blank,** *54 Duke St., W1; tel. 629-3174.*

A few steps down Duke Street from the crushing miracle of Oxford Street, Justin de Blank has been the salvation of many a shopper. The simple cafeteria-style room serves hot dishes, and the menu changes daily: pasta, quiche, vegetarian dishes, salads. The whole wheat breads are the best in London (and served at better restaurants). A surprisingly varied selection of wines is available.

The decor is clean, pleasant, almost minimalist. High rattan booths surround metal tables. Recently, this firm took over the food concession at the National Gallery and the more up-market Tate Gallery.

• **Langan's Brasserie,** *Stratton Street, W1; tel. 493-6437; tube: Green Park.*

This fun, spirited brasserie with David Hockney art on the walls plays nightly host to London's media crowd. Michael Caine is a partner with Irish entrepreneur Peter Langan, whose other successful ventures include Odins. In addition to boasting an exciting atmosphere, the restaurant serves excellent food—and lots of it. The long menu changes daily with the market.

• **Le Gavroche,** *43 Upper Brook St., W1; tel. 408-0881; tube: Bond Street.*

With Tante Claire, Le Gavroche competes for the title of best restaurant in London. A three-star restaurant from the Roux brothers, it has a large menu, and everything on it is good. The cuisine has a bourgeois timbre, heavy on cream and eggs, and you won't go away hungry. Give serious thought to the apricot soufflé—the waiter slits open the top and pours in a mouthwatering apricot sauce. The atmosphere is surprisingly unstuffy, but prices are naturally *haute.* Make reservations in advance. The £19.50 lunch is a legendary deal.

• **Restaurant** and **Grill Room,** *the Connaught, Carlos Place, W1; tel. 499-7070.*

Most go to the Connaught Restaurant for lunch and to the Grill Room for dinner, but both have excellent food. The latter features stuffed birds as part of the decor. Chef Michel Bourdin owns a Michelin star for his marriage of French sauces with English dishes, to wit his sole with two sauces and wild duck with peaches and soft-boiled quail eggs in pastry. The atmosphere—the result of dark woods, old rugs, and cut glass—could not be more English in the best sense.

• **Restaurant,** *the Ritz, Piccadilly, W1; tel. 493-8181; tube: Green Park.*

The Ritz Restaurant occupies the finest dining room in England, adjacent to Green Park, and the food is usually excellent. *Prix-fixe* menus are available at both lunch and dinner. Lunch is cheaper but more difficult to book. The fish sausage is delicious. Service is good. There is really only one Ritz (in London).

• **Terrace** and **Grill Room,** *the Dorchester, Park Lane, W1A2HJ; tel. 629-8888.*

A dance floor, a pianist, and candles provide a romantic setting for the superb cooking served at the Terrace. With two Michelin stars, it is worth a detour, say the tire makers. Swiss chef Anton Mosimann follows the legendary Escoffier's policy of keeping the cooking simple. The halibut with dry cider, for example, is superb. The Grill Room serves crustier fare (such as bread-and-butter pudding) in Spanish surroundings.

Soho

• **Café Pelican,** *45 St. Martin's Lane, WC2; tel. 379-0309.*

Late at night, when few places are open, people are still eating, drinking, and having fun at the Café Pelican. You can meet here before the theater, too, for a drink or coffee. At any hour, the Pelican offers light fare, drinks, and full-course meals. Located a few steps from the London Coliseum, the Pelican is a hangout for performers and theater people. The food is good if not spectacular, the decor pleasant—the restaurant extends way back—and the prices neither expensive nor cheap. This is a valuable institution.

• **Criterion Brasserie/Café,** *222 Piccadilly, W1; tel. 839-7133.*

This simple bistro on Piccadilly Circus has a rich decor and a richer history. Watson, alone in London, met the friend who introduced him to

THE CRITERION BRASSERIE

Sherlock Holmes here, and for many years thereafter the Criterion was a famous watering hole. A no-standing-at-the-bar policy ended a recent vogue, but keeps the place uncrowded. The French food is unpretentious and cheap. More than once at Piccadilly Circus, I've felt the need to sit down, and what could be more convenient?

• **Escargot,** *48 Greek St., W1; tel. 437-2679.*

At Escargot you may eat upstairs among the media types making deals or downstairs, where publishers buy first authors a taste of things to come. Either way you will eat well at reasonable prices. The pasta dishes are a good bet, as is the seafood. Marbled walls and spring colors give an airy cheer to the dining room.

• **Gay Hussar,** *2 Greek St., W1; tel. 437-0973; tube: Tottenham Court Road.*

For years, this restaurant has been the favorite of labor leaders in England, who come here for the good Hungarian cuisine and Victor, the maitre d', a charming Hungarian émigré. At lunchtime, it's difficult to get a table if you're not an MP or a regular, but at night, tables are more readily available, and Victor remains as gracious as ever. Dishes include wild cherry soup, game, and anything you can think of made with paprika. Credit cards are not accepted.

• **Nam Long,** *40 Frith St., W1; tel. 439-1835.*

This small, comfortable room is one of the best Southeast Asian restaurants in London. Although the decor is unremarkable from the outside, inside, the elegant wallpaper and tile floor convey a feeling of well-being. The food is well-prepared, and the sizzling dishes are served in containers set in varnished wood. Try any one of the Vietnamese specialties. The service is attentive, and the restaurant is open until 11 p.m.

• **Rasa Sayang,** *10 Frith St., W1; tel. 734-8720; tube: Tottenham Court Road.*

I first learned to like Indonesian food in Amsterdam, and Rasa Sayang provides a credible London rendition. Spicy coconut and peanut-flavored sauces enliven fresh beef, chicken, and seafood. Rasa Sayang has a strong following among locals.

• **Soho Brasserie,** *23-25 Old Compton St., W1; tel. 439-3758; tube: Leicester Square.*

A few years ago, this place on humble Old Compton Street was *the* place to be seen in London among successful young designers, media types, and models. Today, it's fallen off a tad, but it retains a *fin du monde* energy. At night it reminds me of Rick's Place in *Casablanca,* complete with a French, Bogartesque owner. During a recent visit, I even saw a credible enaction of the pickpocketing scene from the movie—the perpetrator took a bag left by open doors onto the street. Hang on to your belongings, but enjoy the food, the 1920s-style murals, and the ambience.

• **Terrace,** *the Meridien, Piccadilly, W1; tel. 734-8000.*

After the theater, a good place to begin picking apart performances is the Terrace at the Piccadilly Meridien. Once open to guests, the restaurant's outside terrace was a favorite spot for debutantes and their beaus to take some air. Now glassed in and pleasantly decorated, it is packed with businessmen at lunch—who come for the sunlight (on a good day) and the quality of the food. Reservations are not necessary after the theater, and the menu offers full meals, salads, and desserts to accommodate different appetites.

Westminister Abbey and Whitehall

• **Amico,** *44 Horseferry Road, SW1; tel. 222-4680; tube: Westminster.*

A favorite among MPs, who return for votes at the sound of a bell, Amico serves basic Italian food, including spaghetti Gorbachev, created after Labor leader Neil Kinnock brought the reformer here for lunch. At dinner, the parliamentary bustle subsides.

Food to go

• **Fortnum and Mason,** *181 Piccadilly, W2; tel. 734-8040.*

Fortnum and Mason sells almost as much fresh food as Harrods. It excels in pre-packed picnic hampers and tasty jarred or canned chutneys, jams, and puddings. Telephone a day in advance for hampers.

• **Harrods,** *184-210 Brompton Road, Knightsbridge.*

The food halls here are something to behold.

• **Maison Bouquillon,** *41-45 Moscow Road, W2; tel. 229-2107 or 727-4897.*

Here you'll find what are probably the best croissants in London, along with assorted pastries, meats, fish, and cheeses. A take-out *pâtisserie* adjoins a *salon de thé,* where these same creations are available (along with tea and coffee) in a café setting. Try the cheese rolls.

• **Mrs. Stokes' Kitchen,** *1 Kensington Church Walk, W8; tel. 937-9543.*

Hidden up a magical walk, behind St. Mary Abbots Church only a minute from hectic High Street Kensington, Mrs. Stokes' Kitchen serves a potpourri of delicacies, from homemade soups, salads, and cakes to delicious Cajun shepherds pie, bread-and-butter pudding with whiskey sauce, and an unbeatable chicken potpie—most made from produce grown on Mrs. Stokes' own farm in Dorset.

Born in New York, Mrs. Stokes has endeavored to bring a New Yorker's appreciation of fine food to English country fare. As a result, she is in demand as a caterer to dames and lords.

Locals stop in for cappuccino and homemade apple juice. Also good are the fresh Scottish salmon and the homemade preserves (including lemon curd).

• **Partridges,** *132 Sloane St.; tel. 730-0651 or 730-7102.*

Partridges is open from 8:30 a.m. to 9 p.m., seven days a week, serving smoked fish, fresh turkey, ham, beef, cheeses, scones, and quail eggs (which you must cook).

Chapter IV

The next morning I was awakened by a noise in my room. Short tones, one after the other. Short tones that continued on and on like some terrible siren wailing next to my head. I lay still, waiting, but the sounds continued. I reached out my hand and knocked something onto the floor. But at least the tones stopped. I felt relieved and burrowed my head into the feather pillow. From the distant darkness, a dream beckoned. And then, suddenly, I sprang awake. The telephone. I reached over and murmured hello.

"John, I'm so glad I reached you. John, this is Jenny. Jenny Wilde from yesterday."

"Yes. Jenny?"

"I called you last night. Something came up. Please. I have to go away, but I want to see you first. John, when can I see you?"

I kicked away the covers and sat up on the side of the bed.

"Who? Jenny? What's the matter?" It hit me that she had called me John, and now I was calling her Jenny.

"John, I can't talk now. They're right...John, meet me—meet me at the front of Victoria Station, the forecourt, at 1400."

"Jenny, tell me where you are!"

"Please come. I've got to go."

"Jenny!" The phone went dead. I felt dazed. After a moment I called the operator and asked if there was any way to trace a call.

"What?"

"Trace a call." I realized the absurdity of my request. "My...daughter just got cut off and...has no money, and I have to call her back," I dissembled.

"I see, sir. Well, I'll check for you. Do you know where your daughter would have been calling from?"

"No. That's the point."

"I see, of course. Well, I'll check that for you. You're at extension 537? Yes, you are. Very good. I'll call you back."

I hung up the phone and lay back on the bed. My travel alarm clock showed 8 a.m. What a way to start the day. I'd almost forgotten that I had a headache. In fact, I'd almost forgotten everything: the book I was supposed to be writing, my publisher Bill Bonner back in Baltimore. All thoughts of London and writing had flown out of my head with the appearance of Jenny Wilde. Figuratively speaking, of course. Where was she? Why was she so important to me?

Suddenly ravenous, I called room service.

I ordered a bromide, some black coffee, and a full English breakfast—kippers, mushrooms, the works.

"Any papers, sir?" room service asked on the phone.

"Yes, all of them."

"Very good, sir."

A few minutes later, my breakfast and the newspapers arrived. The waiter was all apologies. "I'm sorry, sir. We couldn't find the N*ews of the World*. We sent someone to look for it. We thought they might have it down at..."

"Never mind. It's all right," I said, signing the bill and motioning him off.

The waiter withdrew. I tore first into the Alka Seltzer, then into the stack of seven papers. Those page 3 girls in the *Sun* are something. But nothing new on the MI5 business yesterday. All the papers reported it, but nothing conclusive was mentioned.

A bit later, the phone rang, and the operator apologized for not being able to trace the call. I showered, dressed, and decided to see a bit more of the city before meeting Jenny at Victoria at 2 p.m. Perhaps I was over-reacting.

It was a bright, sunny day. Coming out of the Ritz onto busy St. James's, I walked down toward Jermyn Street. It had been awhile since I'd walked this route, but things were quaintly the same. The famed **Boodles** *(#28)*, **Brooks** *(#61)*, and **Whig and White's** *(#37)* still stared down the street at one another. Farther down, the **Carlton** *(#69)* endured, after having admitted a woman (Margaret Thatcher). **Davidoff** (the cigar store), **Lock** hats, **Lobb** shoes—all were going strong. The **Byron House** *(#7-#9)*, built where Byron woke up famous after penning *Childe Harold,* gave me a momentary thrill. Was it too late for that to happen to me?

My steps took me over to **St. James's Palace,** that sombre

60

St. James's Palace.

bastion of brick. Built by Henry VIII, it was the official palace of kings until succeeded by Buckingham Palace in 1837. Today, the American ambassador is still the ambassador to the court of St. James, though little more than the gatehouse and clock tower remain. Indeed, when the king dies, it is still customary to yell, "The king is dead. Long live the king."

Walking down **King Street,** I passed **Christies** *(#8),* where an auction was in progress. Why not take a gander? Greek statues were on the block. A television camera broadcast them onto monitors throughout the room. On the way out, something caught my eye—a catalog of Egyptian antiquities. "Next week, sir," a gray mustached attendant smiled. I took the catalog and left.

I still had time before my rendezvous with Jenny, so I continued walking. I passed **Berry Brothers,** the wine shop; **Paxton and Whitfield,** the place for cheese; **Floris,** the perfumery; and, of course, the shirtmakers, **Turnbull and Asser.** I came back by **Pall Mall** (which was derived from paille maille, an ancestor of croquet), passing more clubs: **Travelers** *(#106)* and the **Reform** *(#104-#105),* both designed by Barry, who also designed the House of Commons. The Reform was the site of the wager in *80 Days Around the World*; it was also the site of the birth of England's Liberal Party.

What to make of Ms. Jenny Wilde? Really, what had any of this to do with me? She ought to go to the police. That's what I was thinking. I was too old for this sort of thing. I wandered up to Piccadilly, all abuzz at this hour. The Royal Academy was sponsoring a show by Henry Moore (he and Francis Bacon switch off as modern legends—this time it was Moore's turn).

By luck, a **Richoux** turned up at *#172*. Richoux is a good place for a sandwich, a coffee, and a seat when you want to sit down and recharge. Women love Richoux's desserts, which include Death by Chocolate, as well as Richoux's Welsh rarebit, clever salads, and decor. It's a popular place to take a break from shopping. (Another Richoux faces Harrods.) I wolfed down a delicious club sandwich and an expresso and felt my spirits return. A whiskey would have topped things off, but it wasn't on the menu. Fortified, I ventured out into the sunlight and hailed a cab.

"Victoria," I said.

"In a hurry, sir?"

"Yes."

On my way to see Jenny, I thought that perhaps she could be an inspiration for my book (though so far, she'd been only a distraction).

* * *

Well, to interrupt my adventures again and return to the guidebook...

Shopping

If London were famous for nothing else, it would be famous for its shopping. To me, London shops mean tradition, a tradition of quality that goes back centuries (as do many of the stores).

The area of St. James's (from Pall Mall up to Piccadilly, bounded by Green Park to the west and Regent Street to the east) began its history as the back door to St. James's Palace (built by Henry VIII in 1530). Couturiers and other tradesmen naturally located near the palace, where they could best serve their favored clientele, the king, the queen, and the minions. Over the centuries, as the area grew, the shops remained often in their original locations, passed down from generation to generation. As

Regent Street out of Piccadilly Circus.

a result, London's old shops boast an adherence to tradition and quality that you won't find any place else on earth. To give you an example, an American friend of mine went to a famous London tailor to commission an evening suit (or tuxedo) for his wedding back in the United States. The proprietor asked the time of the ceremony. When my friend explained that it was to be a morning wedding, the proprietor refused to sell him the tuxedo, offering instead to make him a morning suit. Tradition dies hard in London.

London is a melting pot of shops and boutiques. About 1,000 London shops possess royal warrants, which you'll see prominently displayed. The warrant means that the shop provides goods to royalty—although not necessarily British (look at the fine print on the seal). Holders of royal warrants "send around" goods to be examined by royalty. The duke or duchess in question takes what he or she wants, paying a price well below list, and sends back the rest. In exchange for the warrant, shopkeepers promise to keep mum on royal habits (so don't bother to ask whether Prince Charles likes striped or plaid pajamas). Royalty may retract the warrant for any reason.

BY APPOINTMENT TO
HER MAJESTY THE QUEEN
COFFEE MERCHANTS

Also lining London's streets are elegant boutiques run by the world's top designers. The city's position as capital of the empire has made it a haven for wealthy visitors, including legions of American tourists visiting the mother country, Arabs (since the 1970s), and plenty of well-heeled Continentals. Most of the top international designers keep shops here, and London's tradition of service assures that these shops are at least on par with those in Paris, Palm Beach, and New York. Quite the opposite of shops selling goods by Appointment to Her Majesty, these boutiques follow the trends in fashion, making a god of the new rather than the old. A stroll down Bond Street reveals such names as Gucci, Giorgio Armani, and Hermes, door to door with Cartier, Dunhill, and Asprey.

Finally, London is also home to shops selling designs of the city's own style (which dates from the 1960s, when Mary Quant set up a shop on King's Road to sell miniskirts). Though the mini today is seen only occasionally, shops on Kensington High Street, Sloane Street, and Beauchamp Place, including Hyper-Hyper, a number of shops near Covent Garden, and the Way In department at Harrods, sell those fur, leather, and psychedelic creations my nephew maintains go well with red and green spiked hair. So much for civilization.

Antiques

• **Bermondsey Market** (or New Caledonian Market), *Bermondsey Square,* on the south side of Tower Bridge Road at Long Lane.

This market is open Friday only, from 6 a.m. to lunchtime.

• **Camden Passage,** *Upper Street, Islington.*

This market is open Wednesday through Saturday. It specializes in books and prints.

Books

• **Cecil Court.**

This tiny street connecting St. Martin's Lane and Charing Cross Road is lined with nothing but bookstores. A must for every bibliophile.

• **Dillons,** *1 Malet St.; tel. 636-1577.*

Dillons specializes in academic books, with a selection rivaling that at Foyles.

• **Foyles,** *113-119 Charing Cross Road.*

The British Museum of bookstores, Foyles could use a new curator. Reputed to have the largest number of books in the world, they are organized by publisher. Question: May I take a look at your books on cricket. Answer: Who published the volume you're looking for? I hurried next door to Waterstones.

- **Francis Edwards,** *48a Charing Cross Road.*

Francis Edwards is another fine dealer of rare books on the Boulevard of Books, Charing Cross Road.

- **Hatchards,** *187 Piccadilly; tel. 439-9921.*

The oldest bookstore in London, Hatchards at Piccadilly is a pleasant place to shop. The wide variety of books is impressive, particularly the collection of books on English specialties, such as gardening, cricket, and travel. Paperbacks are segregated from hardbacks, an example of the class system (of which I approve).

- **Heywood Hill,** *10 Curzon St.; tel. 629-0647.*

A bookstore where the members of the staff have actually read the books and can offer informed opinions to purchasers. Many far-flung Englishmen rely on Heywood Hill for a diet of books from home. Foreigners, too. Although I prefer to select my own books, I enjoy the opportunity to talk over my selections with the witty and capable staff.

- **J.A. Allen,** *1 Lower Grosvenor Place, Buckingham Palace Road; tel. 940-1214 .*

Lovers of horses will find a tremendous selection of books on the equestrian arts at J.A. Allen, which is located behind Buckingham Palace (quite close to its stables).

- **Maggs Brothers Ltd.,** *50 Berkeley Square; tel. 499-2007.*

Maggs Brothers is the finest antiquarian book dealer in London. Occupying a townhouse on giant, leafy Berkeley Square, a Mr. Maggs still

Berkeley Square.

runs Maggs Brothers, which specializes in illuminated manuscripts, first editions, and autographed letters of English authors. Many priceless works are in stock, and the bibliophile (with clean hands) is welcome to stop in to see the treasures. I was overjoyed to inspect one of the original privately printed editions of T.E. Lawrence's (Lawrence of Arabia's) *Seven Pillars of Wisdom.* The lover of fine books will find no worthier shrine.

• **Samuel French Theatre Bookshop,** *52 Fitzroy St.; tel. 387-9373.*

This is where thespians browse and murmur. In addition to playscripts, this shop stocks sound-effects records.

• **Waterstones,** many locations throughout the city, including *121-125 Charing Cross Road.*

This has emerged as the best book chain in London. The selection is extensive, the staff helpful, and the atmosphere literate. Waterstones makes a special effort to stock books by less-known publishers and new authors. Commendable.

• **W.H. Smith,** many locations throughout the city.

The chief virtue of this chain is its numbers. W.H. Smith bookstores are located everywhere.

Cheese

• **Paxton & Whitfield,** *93 Jermyn St.; tel. 930-0250.*

The oldest cheese store in London, Paxton & Whitfield also stocks the greatest variety of cheeses. With more than 300 European cheeses (including some 40 to 50 British ones), Paxton & Whitfield has the cheese you are looking for. Cheeses are stocked not according to price (as in many U.S. cheese shops), but according to tradition. No risk of buying an off-brand wheel of Brie.

Department stores

• **Fortnum and Mason,** *181 Piccadilly.*

Opened in 1707 as a grocery store by William Fortnum, a footman in the household of Queen Anne, Fortnum and Mason is above all famous for its picnic hampers. Not that it doesn't stock women's clothing, china, crystal, antiques, and everything else you'd expect to find in a department store. But the store's hampers have, in that typically British fashion, fed

Wellington's officers on the Peninsula, officers in the Crimean War, and commoners tasting the bounty through pilferage.

Fortnum and Mason's food courts, staffed by salesmen in formal attire treading over plush red carpets, are sure to stir your sense of luxury if not your taste buds. Displayed are jars of marmalade, tins of paté, and cans of tea, stacked, piled, and bundled in ways that promise to solve your gift problems instantly.

For a hamper, order 24 hours ahead. You'll marvel at the basket as well as the food. (Included are disposable forks and plates.) Picnic in a park or head out to a castle in Kent.

For sundaes almost as good as those in America (the sauces and service make up for the watery British ice cream), try Fortnum and Mason's soda fountain (entrance on Jermyn Street). Or better yet have high tea at the St. James's Restaurant on the fourth floor (open from 3 p.m.).

• **Harrods,** *184-210 Brompton Road, Knightsbridge.*

Everyone has heard of Harrods, with its motto "*Omnia, Omnibus, Ubique*" ("All things for all people, everywhere"). Truman Capote bought his hats there. In years gone by, Harrods was also the place to buy an elephant, but the store has trimmed its line considerably, pachyderms apparently gone with India. However, you still can book theater tickets here, have your clothes dry cleaned, borrow a book from the circulating library, and yes, even arrange your funeral.

Whereas at most department stores, you might have to run out to a bank to change money, Harrods has its own (open until 5 p.m.). In addition, an American Express office is located across Brompton Road. Plastic, of course, is welcome.

The Harrods logo looks a bit out of style, but its castle-like terra-cotta building occupying four acres in Knightsbridge, just a few blocks down Brompton Road from Hyde Park, speaks for itself. I like Harrods for the sheer size of the place. The staff is courteous. But what makes the store really notable is that it does have practically everything. The food courts remind you that there is good food in London, even if it doesn't reach the restaurants. The terrace on the fourth floor (by the Georgian Room) is a pleasant place to have tea (£7.20), and on a clear day the view of the neighboring Georgian buildings is straight out of *Mary Poppins.*

- **Liberty,** *210-220 Regent St.*

Notable for the Tudor design of its exterior, Liberty is best-known inside for its wide variety of fabrics—it boasts an entire floor of every color and pattern you can imagine. A selection of pewter fills the top floor; gifts fill the first.

- **Marks and Spencer,** *458 Oxford St.*

A chain of stores, the biggest Marks and Spencer is on Oxford Street, next to Selfridges. All Marks and Spencer merchandise sports the store's own label (St. Michael). Providing sturdy, serviceable goods at good prices, including bargains on sweaters and woolens, Marks and Sparks (as Londonders call it) is England's biggest discount store. Some branches have food courts, where you can stock up on ready-to-eat creations, handy for travelers who like having a bit of food in their hotel rooms.

- **Peter Jones,** *Sloane Square, Chelsea.*

Peter Jones is a much smaller department store than, say, Harrods, but it is a great place to look for linens and housewares, including tea towels and tea caddies, trivet stands, and place mats—even yards of chintz if you are prepared to do your interior decorating in London (remember to bring swatches of what you already have in your room with you).

- **Selfridges,** *400 Oxford St.*

Situated midmarket between Marks and Sparks and Harrods, Selfridges offers designer and other fine goods at lower prices than you'll find at Harrods—however, the selection is also less than at Harrods. Still, this is a civilized place for a man to find a necktie, a shirt, or an evening gown for his lady. My nephew bought a new wristband for his Swatch here.

Guns

In the days of big-game hunting in Africa, London's gun shops provided the firepower necessary to demonstrate white man's mettle. I've always admired George Orwell's account of white man as hunter in *Shooting an Elephant.* Francis Macomber (of the Hemingway story) made the mistake of bolting before a lion, and for that his wife promptly betrayed him. Today, shooting big game is almost entirely illegal. Europeans go to Africa armed with Nikons, not Purdeys.

Nevertheless, a few old shops continue to make exquisite guns, still valuable behind a duck blind, if not from the side of a Land Rover.

However, a bespoke gun, in addition to costing a small fortune, takes several years to make. If you're planning a hunt and need a weapon immediately, the establishments listed below also sell used guns.

To join an English hunt, you need not know how to shoot, but you must be able to ride a horse. The object of a hunt is to follow on horse your hounds, who chase and devour the foxes. The footman may engage in beagling, whereby you follow your beagles, who likewise devour your prey. Pick up a copy of *Horse and Hound* to learn more.

- **Holland & Holland,** *33 Bruton St., off Bond Street.*

This firm runs a shooting school in addition to its gun shop. (The school, *Duck's Hill Road, Northwood, Middlesex HA62SS; tel. 65-274-25349,* caters to beginners as well as professionals.) Holland & Holland sells royal double-barreled guns, big-game rifles, revolvers, and Cavalier boxlocks. The waiting time for a handmade gun is up to three years. The store also stocks a wide variety of accessories, from books to clothing to dog whistles.

- **James Purdey & Sons,** *57-58 S. Audley St.*

All you could ask of a gun shop. Again, a bespoke gun will take several years to make. A superb line of accessories.

- **William Evans,** *67a St. James's St.; tel. 493-0415.*

William Evans makes two guns: best sidelock and best boxlock, both based on a Mauser action. You can opt for a scope, a drop trigger, or personalized engraving. Expect about a two-year wait for the finished product.

Hats

- **James Lock & Company,** *6 St. James's St.*

The country that perfected the raincoat and the umbrella has, not surprisingly, also done a great deal for the hat. Once upon a time, it was common to wear a top hat in London,

69

thanks to James Lock, who invented them. Today, hats are much more popular in the country. And the place to get them is James Lock & Company—anything from Cokes (that is, Bowlers—Mr. Bowler made this famous hat for Mr. Coke) to Homburgs to riding and polo hats. The firm uses a conformateur that exactly measures the head. The resulting fit is virtually perfect.

Perfume

• **Floris & Company Perfumers,** *89 Jermyn St.*

Perfume has never been a British art. Like women's fashion, perfumery took a second seat here to services for men. As a result, a gathering of British women has never meant the same bouquet of scents you can expect to enjoy at a gathering of women in France. Nevertheless, few women can resist the delights of Floris & Company. What the scents here lack in secret ingredients to bewitch the race of men, they make up in simple, natural variety.

The shop opened as a distiller of the essences of flowers, and its fragrances still correspond to flowers. As is usual in the best English shops, Floris maintains a record of customer preferences to use when filling future orders.

In addition to perfumes, Floris stocks soaps, salts, combs, and brushes, including shaving things for men. I have never adjusted to shaving with foam from a can, and to this day I use a shaving brush and soap. I bought my last badger-hair brush at Floris, and it has served (and lathered) me well.

Raincoats

• **Aquascutum,** *100 Regent St.*

Aquascutum, one of London's big names, made raincoats for the British army during World War II. The store also stocks a full line of fine British clothing.

• **Burberrys,** many locations throughout the city, including *18-22 Haymarket St.*

Most consider Burberrys *the* raincoat maker. The store also sells other good clothing (not necessarily with the famous Burberry plaid).

Shirts

• **Harvie & Hudson,** *77* and *96-97 Jermyn St.*
Harvie & Hudson sells first-rate traditional shirts.
• **Turnbull & Asser,** *71 Jermyn St.; tel. 930-0502.*
This shop makes what most people will tell you are the best shirts on Jermyn Street.
• **Sale Shop,** *155 Oxford St., 2 St. Barnabas St., and 5 Park Walk.*
Shop here for big discounts on traditional shirts and other clothing. Don't expect big names, but the quality is generally good.

Shoes

• **Blackman's Shoe Shop,** *28a Cheshire St.; tel. 739-3902.*
This is where I buy my shoes, or at least some of them. Dirt cheap (as little as £20) but good quality. An English tradition—at least for me.
• **Church's,** *163 New Bond St.*
Here you'll find the well-known brand name at prices well below those in the United States.
• **John Lobbs,** *9 St. James's St.*
It will take you six months to have a pair of shoes made at Lobbs, but the finished product may last you a lifetime. Lobb shoes are known for durability more than style—although you can have a pair custom-made according to any design you can think of. And when it comes time to resole, Lobbs actually prefers you send the shoe back to its staff for meticulous attention. The shop is dark, heady, almost a bit down-at-heel, but quite gentlemanly, and it smells of thick, oily leathers—as befits a shoe shop.

Most of the work is done on the premises. Once you select a style, a series of craftsmen attends to your shoes, from the fitter who fits them to the clicker who cuts the uppers to the last-maker to the closer to the maker. You can choose brogues, Oxfords, Monks, or Norwegians—or from a great variety of boots. Velvet slippers monogrammed in gold are a specialty. I would have shoes made here if I could afford it.

• **Trickers,** *67 Jermyn St.*
A block down, nestled among the shirtmakers, Trickers is a venerable shoemaker to the gentry.

• **Wildsmith,** *Prince's Arcade, Piccadilly.*

This fine old shop off Piccadilly is rather less expensive than Lobbs, but it makes an excellent and dependable shoe.

Specialty shops

• **Anything Left-Handed Ltd.,** *65 Beak St.*

For the left-handed among us.

• **Arthur Middleton,** *12 New Row, Covent Garden; tel. 836-7042.*

This is the place for antique scientific instruments. Beautiful and expensive; however, at Christmas, Mr. Middleton stocks a few less expensive items. The antique medical instruments (leech jars, mechanical drills) are popular gifts for doctors.

• **Asprey,** *165-169 New Bond St.; tel. 493-6767.*

Very pricey gifts.

• **Constant Sale Shop,** *56 Fulham Road.*

Designer clothing on sale. Run by a man with other designer stores, the Constant Sale Shop is his outlet.

• **Davenport's,** *51 Great Russell St.*

This world-class joke shop takes inspiration from the British Museum across the street.

• **General Trading Company,** *144 Sloane St., Sloane Square; tel. 730-0411.*

Pricey but beautiful gifts. This is where Lady Di registered her wedding list.

Smithfield Market.

• **Hyper-Hyper,** *26-40 Kensington High St.*

Hyper-Hyper is a collection of designer stalls all in one giant hall. Post-punk trendy (however, I'm told that recently an element of classicism has crept into this shrine to the outrageous).

• **Irish Linen Company,** *35-36 Burlington Arcade; tel. 493-8949.*

The Irish Linen Company has a good selection of the finest linens in the world.

• **Kite Store,** *69 Neal St.; tel. 836-1666.*

When the sky is gray, visit the Kite Store for a bit of color.

• **Prestat,** *40 S. Molton St.*

Good chocolates, including Paddington the Bear.

• **Reject China Shop,** *33-35 Beauchamp Place.*

The Reject Shop has good deals on china—pieces are generally 20% less than in other shops.

• **Savoy Taylors Guild,** *164 New Bond St.* and *93-95 the Strand.*

The Savoy Taylors Guild is a men's store in Mayfair with uncommonly good sale prices on the best designer merchandise.

• **Sulka,** *19 Old Bond St.*

While Sulka makes a variety of luxury clothing, it is the last word in monogrammed silk robes—which cost from $2,000. Sulka is for those who can afford the *ne plus ultra*.

Sports

• **Lillywhites,** *Piccadilly Circus.*

Cricket bats, rugby shirts—everything for the athlete.

Stationery

• **Chisolm's,** four locations, including *20 Lincoln's Inn Fields; tel. 430-1651.*

The filofax, like Burberry and Aquascutum raincoats, owes its existence to World War II. Developed for officers to keep personnel reports and to maintain track of artillery throw weights, the filofax languished in military corridors and stuffy briefcases before being rediscovered a few years ago. For years, Chisolm's was the only place to buy a filofax, but

73

today the books are available everywhere, even given away in promotions.

• **Falkiner's Fine Papers,** *117 Long Acre, Covent Garden; tel. 240-2339.*

Falkiner's has more than 1,000 kinds of paper, gold leaf, and the finest India inks.

• **Ryman,** many locations throughout the city.

A convenient place to buy pads, pens, ribbons, diskettes—and the famous filofax.

• **Smythson of Bond Street,** *54 New Bond St.; tel. 629-8558.*

Well before filofax, there was what was in many ways a better product. For years, Smythson has been making a diary that fits in your pocket and barely disturbs the lines of your suit. By using blue paper instead of white, the 19th-century founder realized he could use a thinner grade of paper (because writing does not show through the blue). His store has prospered ever since, overseeing the marriage of leather and paper. In addition to diaries, address books, and blotters, this store also stocks a fine line of papers, envelopes, and cards. Good ink and paper make you write better.

Suits

A bespoke suit should last you a lifetime. Though considerably more expensive than one off the rack, the quality, fit, and classic styling promise a better investment in the long run.

While Savile Row tailors strive to accommodate customer preferences in such matters as cuffs, fob pockets, and cloth, most have a clear signature style. If you like well-padded shoulders and a dropped waist, you should walk two blocks over from Savile Row to Bond Street and stop in at Giorgio Armani or Emmanuel Ungaro.

On the other hand, if you like a classic English cut, you can do no better (and pay no more) than at the shops listed below. Tommy Nutter, Blades, and Paul Smith offer the greatest choices in design.

Keep in mind that you probably will require two fittings at some distance apart (the first usually takes place when you choose the fabric). Unless you are living in London, you will need to make two trips or take advantage of the tailor's trips to America (see Stovel & Mason). Savile Row tailors welcome Americans. Royal warrants notwithstanding, about half their business comes from American businessmen.

- **Anderson & Sheppard,** *30 Savile Row.*

Anderson & Sheppard makes soft suits with a minimum of lining and padding, for a soft, smooth appearance. If, unlike the Prince of Wales, you don't favor this natural look, you should look elsewhere.

- **Blades of Savile Row,** *8 Burlington Gardens.*

Japanese punk at a highbrow address. Blades carries a variety of flamboyant high-style accessories—although the suits are more traditional. Expect to pay at least £1,000 for one.

- **H. Huntsman & Sons,** *11 Savile Row, W1.*

The top Savile Row tailor according to many—and usually the most expensive. I like the look of Huntsman's suits—a minimum of padding and pockets, shoulders cut square, jacket flared at the waist—but I can't say that I own one. A good selection of fabrics, including the heavier wools. A suit runs about £1,200.

- **Kilgour, French & Stanbury Ltd.,** *8 Savile Row.*

A well-known off-the-rack name in the United States, Kilgour, French & Stanbury makes bespoke suits in London. New Yorkers will appreciate that the firm has a New York branch, where alterations can be done.

- **Paul Smith,** *43-44 Floral St., Covent Garden; tel. 379-7133.*

Paul Smith makes traditional suits with a slight flair. He uses the odd detail to give his work a unique, more contemporary look. Appropriately, he is located on Floral Street, traditionally a street for those things associated with the art of dance, not on Saville Row.

- **Stovel & Mason Ltd.,** *32 Old Burlington St.; tel. 734-4855.*

Good prices on very good bespoke suits. The king of Greece was a customer. Suits here are about half the price of those at H. Huntsman. The owner, Ian Gregorson, visits New York several times a year—so you may be able to schedule one of your fittings there.

- **Tommy Nutter,** *18-19 Savile Row; tel. 734-0831.*

One of the stars of the 1960s, Tommy Nutter still dresses pop stars—but now he designs for various lords as well. Elton John is

A market in the City.

75

a regular patron. You'll probably recognize the look from high-fashion magazines: square-shouldered, ventless jackets and baggy, high-cut trousers (although Nutter has toned it down a bit in recent years). Unlike most of his peers on Savile Row, Nutter will design a suit for you personally in any of a wide variety of fabrics. I couldn't wear one, but many young lords do.

Sweaters

London has no shortage of fine woolens, but you could spend months finding the cheapest place to buy them. Don't waste your time. The following (with Marks and Spencer) offer the best prices on quality sweaters (which in Britain are called cardigans or pullovers).

• **Irish Shop,** *11 Duke St.; tel. 935-1366,* and *80 Buckingham Gate; tel. 222-7132.*

A full range of fine Irish goods, from Irish hand-cut crystal to linen to tweeds. This is the place to shop if you can't make it to Ireland.

• **Portobello China & Woollens Ltd.,** *89 Portobello Road.*

Near the market on Portobello Road (and mobbed on Saturday), this store offers good deals on label-less sweaters. While Westaway sells traditional items, Portobello sells designer merchandise, some of it seconds. The staff generally will tell you what is what, but look carefully. The big discounts do not apply to china.

• **Westaway & Westaway,** *62-65 Great Russell St.*

A warren of townhouses opposite the British Museum offers a neat but rambling assortment of wool goods, including a great variety of sweaters. The sweaters shop has five rooms, including one secreted away in the back. Sale goods are on the bottom shelves downstairs.

Tobacco

I don't normally smoke cigars, but there's something about the chance to enjoy the best of anything. The best cigars in the world are from Cuba. Don't think of bringing any home, its illegal to import Cuban cigars into the United States. But while in London, stop in Dunhill's or Robert Lewis and sample the best: Bolivar, Montechristo, El Ray del Mundo. Dunhill's, of course, sells much else that is good.

• **Alfred Dunhill's,** *30 Duke St., St. James's.*

The largest and original shop is on Duke Street, but smaller branches are peppered throughout the city. Dunhill's is a treasure-trove of tobacco, leather, and cloth. A solid gold lighter is about $5,000, but others are more modestly priced. Upstairs is the humidor room, where, in addition to cigars, you can select a custom blend of tobacco, which the store will record for future reference. You also can choose from pipes, watches, luggage, and clothing. Dunhill's makes me think of empire. I have a Dunhill blazer that has lasted forever—yes, I'm that old—and never creases, a blessing in my business.

- **Robert Lewis,** *19 St. James's St.*

Cigars, cigars, cigars. And snuff.

Toys

- **Hamleys,** *188 Regent St.; tel. 734-3161.*

Hamleys is the world's largest toy store. Bigger than New York's FAO Schwartz. I felt at home here.

Umbrellas

- **James Smith & Sons,** *53 New Oxford St.; tel. 836-4731.*

A Mrs. May O'Sullivan hand-sewed umbrellas for this firm for more than 55 years, perfecting the difficult art. Such luminaries as Gladstone and Lord Curzon kept dry with Smith umbrellas, and the firm supplied countless swagger sticks to British officers during World War I. Smith & Sons continues to make one of the finest umbrellas in London.

- **Swaine, Adeney, Briggs & Sons,** *185 Piccadilly.*

Smith's chief competition, Swaine, Adeney, Briggs & Sons enjoys the advantage of the royal warrant. The firm began in 1750 making whips. In the same location more than 200 years later, the firm's whips are still famous, as are its Briggs umbrellas, walking sticks, and saddlery. You can order a walking stick here with a watch, a flask, or even a .410 shotgun built in. As for umbrellas, the sky is truly the limit. All are hand-sewn and of similar design, but you can choose from silk, crocodile, or lizard and, for the handle, anything from leather to malacca to ivory. The firm also stocks clothing, guns, and playing cards. When it rains, it pours.

Wine

- **Berry Brothers & Rudd Ltd.,** *3 St. James's St.*

Installed in the same premises since 1731, Berry Brothers is the perfect example of a London luxury store. Broad elm board floors, oak paneling, and the careful attentions of the staff make buying good wine as fun as drinking it (almost). When you enter the store, you may be struck, as I always am, by the giant scale. Built to weigh sacks of coffee, it has in fact weighed the likes of Lord Byron, Napoleon III, and Beau Brummel, whose avoirdupois have been recorded in a series of weighty tomes. Humans have grown heavier over the years, including me, and I did not request the privilege of joining those ranks. Instead, I ordered some fine claret and an excellent bottle of sherry. I have been on Berry Brothers' mailing list for many years, and I suggest you sign up as well.

- **Green's,** *34 Royal Exchange.*

Whereas Berry Brothers caters to gentlemen in St. James's, Green's has served habitués of the city for more than two centuries. In addition to a full line of wines, Green's stocks a wide variety of cigars. What's more, Green's runs a wine investment program—whereby you can buy by the cask. The knowledgeable staff will discuss it with you.

- **John Harvey & Sons Ltd.,** *27 Pall Mall.*

Speaking of wine, Harvey & Sons (of Bristol renown) is known for its sherries and its ports. Less atmosphere, though, than Berry Brothers.

- **Oddbins,** *141 Nottinghill Gate; tel. 229-4082, and 142 Fulham Road; tel. 373-5715.*

Despite the lore of the above-mentioned shops, most Londoners buy at Oddbins, a large, well-stocked chain. Prices are good, and the staff is generally helpful. Oddbins reminds me of Astor Liquor in New York.

Women's fashions

Women will find it more difficult to outfit themselves in London than men. If you are too old to wear the lace and ruffles of Laura Ashley, you must content yourself with tweeds and cashmere sweaters, the English country house look (which unfortunately looks better on houses than on women). The best buy is probably shearing (sheepskin), which is currently ultra-fashionable. Lady Di and the Sloane Rangers began this mode.

The following is a rundown of the best London has to offer in the way of women's fashion (at least as far as I could determine). When shopping, keep in mind that British ladies' sizes are less flattering than American. A U.S. size 12 probably will require a British size 14.

• **Browns,** *23-27 S. Molton St.; tel. 491-7833,* and *6c Sloane St.; tel. 493-4232* or *734-4060.*

Browns offers probably the most elegant selection of women's clothing in town. The store chooses the best of various designers' offerings to make its own collection. Most of the big names are here.

• **Harvey Nichols,** *109 Knightsbridge, near Harrods.*

This shop offers clothes with a less sporty look than most British ladies go in for. Prices are steep, but the quality tends to make it worthwhile.

• **Laura Ashley,** many locations throughout the city, including *208 Regent St.*

English country prints incorporated into clothing, draperies, and fabrics. A kind of pastoral, dreamy innocence in all the ruffles, lace, and frills. The close-out bins sometimes hold incredible bargains—particularly on fabrics.

• **Liberty of London,** *Regent Street.*

Rather improbably, Liberty of London is a good source for knockoffs of the designs of *haute couture.* This shop copies whatever the French are showing during any particular season—and so far has managed to brush off lawsuits for copyright infringement from across the Channel.

If you consider Her Majesty a fashion plate, this is the place to shop. Liberty of London's home-grown couturier, Norman Hartnell, dresses the queen. And the queen's daughters-in-law, who started marriage with a bit of flair, are gradually being turned into right royal frumps under the guidance of this designer (in my view).

• **Marks and Spencer,** *458 Oxford St.*

This is the place for women's underwear and sweaters in standard colors. While in England, you may be embarrassed by your too-obvious standard-issue Marks & Sparks knitwear, but once you have crossed the Atlantic, your import will become unusual.

Marks and Sparks underwear is a European bargain; chic ladies from Paris and the Middle East come to London to stock up on lacy little nothings from the firm's Oxford Street flagship.

• **Rayne,** many locations throughout the city, including two shops on *Oxford Street,* shops all over smart *High Street, 15 Old Bond St.,* and *57 Brompton Road.*

Rayne is where the queen purchases her shoes. She goes in for a standard pump with a little bow or rosette on the front and a graceful low heel. And Rayne makes this shoe in every color of the rainbow. Members of the royal family are on their feet a lot—what better recommendation for a pair of shoes?

In the case of shoes, British sizing is more flattering than American. Most women wear British shoes that are two sizes smaller than their American counterparts (if you wear a 7 in the United States, you will need a 5 in Britain). Unlike shoes of the Continent, which often are not available in varying widths, the British, like Americans, have narrow feet and make their shoes in widths from AA to D (again, these do not correspond to American sizes).

• **Sheepskin Shop,** *435-437 Oxford St.*

This is a good source of chic shearing.

Shopping districts

If you're in the mood for shopping, but you're not looking for anything in particular, take a walk through one of the following areas of the city, where you can window shop to your heart's content (and do some sightseeing at the same time).

• **Fulham Road and Brompton Cross.** From Park Walk to Beaufort Street along Fulham Road is the Strip, or Sloane Ranger heaven. Here the trendier Sloane Rangers attend movies at the cinema on the corner of Drayton Gardens, stroll up and down the street, and sip exotic cocktails at the many mediocre restaurants. Savvy Sloane Rangers hang out at the downstairs bar of Blakes Hotel (where Mick Jagger stays).

Shopping addicts shouldn't miss the stretch of Fulham Road that runs from Elm Park Gardens down to the Bibendum Building (formerly the Michelin Building), which houses offices of Michelin's various businesses and an up-market furniture store.

When making your way down the street, look in **Butler and Wilson,** where Di and Fergie buy their costume jewelry, and at the pottery in **J.K. Hill.**

If you're hungry, stop at **Joe's Café,** *126 Draycott Ave.* (open until 11:30 p.m.), one of London's hottest eateries. Joe's is inexpensive for this area and a good place to have steak *frites* or a salad. Alternatively, try **51**, for the best Cajun food in London, or **Ma Cuisine,** *113 Walton St.,* both open at mealtimes only.

If you make reservations in advance (two weeks for dinner; three or four days for lunch) you can dine at the ultra-chic **Bibendum,** *81 Fulham Road,* upstairs in the Bibendum Building. The food is good (no stars from Michelin), the prices high, and the atmosphere bright and open. However, the slightly snobbish nature of the staff may put you off, as it did me. An alternative is to have a drink (served with hot French bread on weekdays) at the pleasant bar downstairs, then move on to continue your shopping down humble—but expensive—Fulton Road.

• **Kensington Church Walk.** Only steps from the exhaust and raging traffic of Kensington High Street is one of the most beautiful places in London, known as Kensington Church Walk.

At the intersection of Kensington High Street and Kensington Church Street, known as High Street-Ken and Church Street-Ken, respectively, is **St. Mary Abbots Church.** Thomas Hardy worshipped here, and it is worth admiring. On the left (or High Street) side of the church is a small door. Walk through the cloistered corridor along the side of the church, and you are transported back to medieval London. Above the school on the left, a painted boy and girl look out onto the square, where many of the faithful are buried. Continuing back, you come to Kensington Church Walk (on your right) and a little park frequented by a few savvy office workers at lunchtime. They buy delicious lunches at **Mrs. Stokes' Kitchen,** *1 Kensington Church Walk,* and enjoy a medieval interlude on their lunch hours.

Turn right up the walk, and you come to the a jewelry store specializing in African-inspired creations made of ivory, ebony, and turquois. The creations cost from a few pounds to almost £1,000.

From here, a small court extends to the left. Ezra Pound lived at *#10* (you may wish you did, too). The doll shop at *#17* is open by appointment only. A few steps up the walk is Mrs. Stokes' Kitchen. Just behind her shop, in a hidden courtyard, is the **China Repair Shop,** a wonderfully ancient London workshop, where china is lovingly made and restored by ladies who have been doing this work for decades.

Continuing up the walk takes you to Holland Street. From there I suggest that you retrace your steps back down and around the park, which will bring you back to High Street-Ken and civilization.

• **Mayfair.** Mayfair is London's finest quarter, home to Claridge's, Brown's, and most of the city's finest hotels. The prime shopping area is along Bond Street, New and Old, in the arcades, Burlington and Prince's, along Savile Row, and on Piccadilly. Right in the middle of it all is the Royal Academy, which puts on some of London's best art exhibits (as I mentioned above, this is where I saw Henry Moore). Across from Mayfair is St. James's.

• **St. James's.** Piccadilly is the home of Fortnum and Mason, Hatchards (for books), and numerous other stores, but the main drags in this area are Jermyn Street (famous for its shirts), which runs just below Piccadilly, and St. James's Street, home of dealers to Britain's gentle class. St. James's is also where you will find many of the city's best clubs.

• **South Molton Street.** At first glance, this area appears a rather tawdry pedestrians-only mall. Actually, however, it is the home of some of the city's finest designer boutiques. Browns designer department store is here, as is Valentino's Oliver line. Also look for **Bazaar**, *1* and *4 S. Molton St.; tel. 499-3127*, which stocks giant square-toe boots, Sergeant Pepper jerkins, and John Paul Gaultier clothing. (I probably wouldn't have gone in, but I didn't want to let my more adventurous readers down.)

At the top of the street, by the Bond Street tube, is a pub where young people congregate after shopping at the less expensive stores on the block, such as Benetton and Cacherel.

Chapter V

No sooner had I stepped from my cab at Victoria Station and walked a half-dozen steps than I saw Jenny approaching me pushing a luggage cart. She wore a comely Burberrys trench coat and scarf and looked just as attractive as I remembered her.

"C'mon!"

"Where are we going?"

"To get a cab."

"The line's over there."

"Don't be daft," she snapped. "And take this."

I obliged by taking charge of the cart. A few steps outside the station we found a taxi right away, and I saw her reason for eschewing the line. We climbed in, and I swung her large leather satchel in between us.

"Westminster," she said, as I tried to move the satchel onto the floor. She put out a hand to help me lower it down.

"I thought you were going away," I said.

She stared at me, her blue eyes unnaturally bright. "I'm glad to see you. You won't believe this, but I have to leave, and...there's something I have to ask you." She paused, staring out the window as the cab swept up Victoria. "Shall we look in at Westminster Abbey?"

"Westminster Abbey?"

"You're going to put that in your book, aren't you? Don't you want a tour?"

"Of Westminster? Why not? But what's with the leather bag?"

"That...is a few of my things. You'll keep them for me, won't you, John?"

"You don't need them?"

"Not for now."

"You are going away."

"Right here," she called to the driver.

83

"I'll tell you inside." We got out, and she motioned for me to pay. The driver was the picture of discretion. I had no idea what to make of this. I dropped the bag and reached for my wallet.

"Careful!" Her eyes followed the bag. "That bag contains old belongings...of my mother's."

"I'm sorry."

"It's OK," she said. "C'mon." And we entered Westminster Abbey.

Much of London is technically part of Westminster City. When Edward the Confessor completed Westminster Abbey in 1065, this area was little more than pasture upstream from the ancient Roman city of Londinium. But when William the Conqueror chose the abbey for his coronation, he began a tradition. Every monarch, except Edward V and Edward VII, has been crowned here, and through this patronage, Westminster has grown.

Queen Victoria receiving the Sacrament after her coronation in Westminster Abbey, June 28, 1838.

With the Reformation, the abbey became first a cathedral of the Church of England, then a Royal Peculiar (a church belonging to the state), which was an interesting solution to the church-state problem. It was while resisting the power of the state that Archbishop Thomas à Becket and Sir Thomas More lost their heads. The triumph of the state with respect to Westminster is evident in the plethora of national figures buried inside, which Jenny pointed out as I followed her, carrying her leather bag.

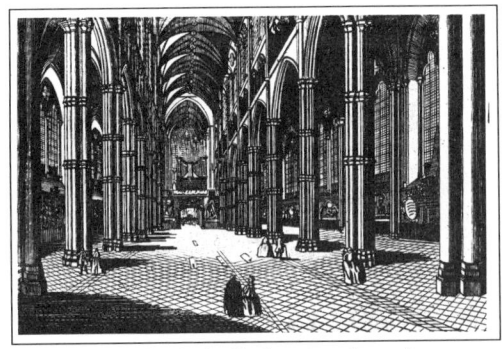

Indeed, so many great people are buried here that they lie vertically in some places. We passed the tombs of Sir Isaac Newton, Jane Austen, Thomas Hardy, Charles Dickens, Thomas Browning—an honor roll of literature. Elizabeth Barrett Browning did not make it. Here are all the kings you could imagine, along with a good measure of noblemen and prime ministers. The Tomb of the Unknown Soldier is here. Poet's Corner is the final resting place of Chaucer, but memorializes many other poets as well, including Coleridge and T.S. Eliot. Byron, though, was excluded, for misbehavior.

Westminster Abbey is the final resting place of centuries' accumulation of illustrious Britons.

As we passed the other tourists, I tried to make heads or tails of Jenny's behavior. We visited the Abbey Museum, where royal effigies used in lying-in-state ceremonies remain. All the while, Jenny remained utterly professional—I wondered if at the end of the tour she would ask me to pay her.

"Admiral Nelson, there, do you know his effigy was considered unnaturally accurate?" I looked down at a reasonably well-preserved specimen of the seafarer.

"You see, his mistress arranged his hair."

We left this exhibit and passed through several chapels. At last we paused in the ancient College Garden by the Dean's Yard, both part of Westminster School, a private boys' high school, the oldest in Britain.

"John, you'll have to forgive me all this, but I'm in...in deep trouble. I believe there are people following me. That's why I just put on this show. In case they're watching us, they'll think I'm giving you a tour."

85

"Who?"

"I can't say. Just please take care of this bag until I come back."

"How will I reach you?"

"You won't. I'll reach you. If anyone asks, you know nothing about me. And by all means don't let anyone have that bag—if you do, I'll be in danger."

"But how will you reach me?"

"Don't worry. I'll meet you at one of these tourist places."

"When?"

"Well, say a week. Next Sunday. At the boat house in Hyde Park at 2."

"OK."

"John."

"What?" She stared deep into my eyes. She reached up, grabbed my head, and kissed me for an incredible half-minute. Then she turned and ran out. I stood there, stupidly. By the time I regained enough sense to follow her, she was gone.

Wandering away from the abbey, a bit dazed, I made my way past Parliament to the little park known as **Victoria Gardens** on the bank of the Thames. I took a chair near a casting of Rodin's *The Burghers of Calais* and tried to think things over.

Parliament sits on the site of the old Palace of Westminster. Most of the palace burned in the fire of 1834, as recorded by Turner and Constable in sketchbooks. The new buildings, built by the classicist Barry and gilded by the medievalist Pugin, were painted everlastingly by Monet. They remain a symbol of England. The best view is of Monet's work, as seen from the bridge or from south of the river, but the side view from the park is nice, too.

The clock tower on the far side houses **Big Ben,** which is actually a bell, named for corpulent Sir Benjamin Hall, public works commissioner during its casting. When it is lit up, it means that Parliament is in session. If you'd like to see the parliamentary process in action, either contact the U.S. embassy, which has an allotment of tickets to the Strangers Gallery (and a waiting list of up to a month) or simply go in person after 4:45 p.m., when the Lower House of Parliament is usually still in session. After the theater, some Londoners have their cabs swing by Parliament. If the light is on, it can make an amusing nightcap. If you have a chance, suggest meeting an MP for a beer on the terrace. Guy Fawkes Day, the British fireworks day (similar to our Fourth of July), was named for a Catholic who tried to blow these buildings up.

North lie the government buildings collectively known as **Whitehall** (after the palace formerly located there). Considered monstrously ugly, most people were glad the original palace burned in 1698, prompting the royal migration to St. James's and later Buckingham. Most visitors to the city also like to take a look at the **Banquet House,** built by Inigo Jones; **Scotland Yard** (though the police moved out long ago); and **10 Downing St.,** the office of the prime minister.

Quaint, narrow Downing Street is now off-limits to tourists, but you can see about all there is to see from the corner of Whitehall. The **War Rooms** (Clive Steps, King Charles Street) served as the nerve center for Winston Churchill in the dark days of World War II. At the gate to what's left of the palace, a poorly dressed guard inspects the troops at 11 a.m. (10 a.m. on Sunday)—this is worth watching if you're there, and it's less crowded than the changing of the guard at Buckingham Palace.

10 Downing St.

At the top of Whitehall (and Trafalgar Square) is the **National Gallery,** strongest in early Italian works and Hogarth. The fellow on the column in the middle of Trafalgar is Lord Nelson (again). At the rear of the National Gallery is the **National Portrait**

Gallery, which displays England's history in faces. But all these I left for later. I had little appetite for them now.

Walking around the garden was a skinhead I found rather unsettling. Rising from my bench, I headed in no particular direction, lugging the leather satchel, until convinced the skinhead was no longer following me. I decided I ought to put the sack in my room. When I got there, I was tempted to open the bag. But no, better to know little.

Trafalgar Square.

The next day I moved out of the Ritz and into the Savoy for a change of pace. I stowed Jenny's suitcase in my closet, covered it with a blanket, and got on with the important things in life. Sipping scotch while looking out at the fabulous vista my art-deco room afforded from our bend in the **River Thames.**

The Thames is a wide river. It is a working river, even today. This thought hit me one afternoon as I watched the sun glimmer over its surface, sparkling with the occasional passing of barges, from my comfortable period armchair. It is not what it was when Engels wrote,

> *I know nothing more imposing than the view which the Thames affords when you sail up the river from the sea toward London Bridge. The masses of houses, the wharves on both sides, the countless ships: it is all so magnificent, on such a massive scale, that you are quite lost in astonishment at the greatness of England even before treading on English soil.*

No, it is no longer quite that. But at that moment it did seem what Churchill called "the silver thread that runs through the history of England." The mighty, sleepy, roaring Thames that has taken out many a body with the tide—if you put any stock in Dickens or Doyle.

I resolved the following day to make my way to **Greenwich** and the **National Maritime Museum**—to face England's nautical history straight on. I would advise every traveler to do precisely this upon arriving in England. For the connection to the sea lies at the root of the country's history.

I made it a full-fledged outing. Alas, I would have liked very much to call Jenny, but I had to find someone else. I tried Jim MacAllister, but he was busy. At last I found an old friend with some time on his hands, Nigel Turbull, the actor. If you've never heard of him, I'm not surprised; but Nigel is a respected name in the theater. Actually, he coaches Shakespeare more than he acts—the call of the Bard is eternal.

Nigel stopped by my rooms, and we took a cab down to Tower Hill, where, Nigel explained, you catch the Docklands Light Railway. Our plan was to go to the Docklands first, then take the foot tunnel under the water and return by boat. Along the way, Nigel pointed out some of the more interesting things in the neighborhood.

As we came out of the Savoy drive, Nigel gestured down the block to the **Coutts Bank,** where the royal family keeps its money. Our cab swept around Aldwych, and all at once we were on Fleet Street. We passed Old Bailey and the law courts, where many famous criminals have been tried. A short way down is the famous **Temple Bar**—which marks the border between Westminster and the City.

"That's where they used to stick the heads of traitors," Nigel noted pleasantly. "And there's the Wig and Pen."

He pointed to a ramshackle club popular among journalists and lawyers. Off to our right, Nigel noted, out of sight on the river, was the Inner Temple, where barristers keep their offices.

The legal system in England is split in two. Clients deal with solicitors, who in turn deal with an elect group of barristers, who alone and bewigged may plead cases in court. All belong to one of four Inns of Court. The system is analogous to that among stock traders before the Big Bang abolished the distinction. There is a movement to do the same for lawyers.

From the legal end of the street, we passed to the domain of journalists. What a sad transition—for virtually all the papers are gone. Of course, Fleet Street was never known for telling the truth. Lies and scandal were its specialties. Nor for some time has the English press been English-owned. Australian Rupert Murdoch now owns the giant *Sun,* with its subscription of more than four million, the *Times,* and several other papers. He bought the *Times* from the Thomson family of Canada. The flight from Fleet Street to the Docklands, spearheaded by Murdoch, has ended an era.

We passed **El Vino's,** the famous Fleet Street watering hole, and Nigel pointed out the **Cheshire Cheese** (down an alley), where Dr. Johnson drank. (His house, where he completed the first English dictionary, is nearby, at *17 Gough St.*)

Then, leaving Fleet Street behind, we passed into the City proper, that part of London synonymous with finance. The buildings are not as tall as those on Wall Street, but the effect is the same. Everywhere I saw men in suits (fewer women than in America), hurrying about between buildings. If there is a difference between the City and Wall Street, it's that London's financial district adheres to decorum. Everyone looks the part. Messengers don't scream curses at truck drivers, and construction workers don't dare to make catcalls. They are all strictly loyal to the gentry—that's the effect of the class system.

"All the world's a stage," that's what I always think in the City," Nigel commented. "So many players, dealing commodities, like so many merchants before them. A never-ending pageant, an elaborate processional staged by Mammon."

We continued on past **St. Paul's Cathedral** perhaps—more than Westminster Abbey—London's greatest cathedral.

"It was almost alone in surviving the bombing," Nigel explained. "All the new buildings you see, they were built over the rubble."

During the Blitz, the East End was by far the hardest hit, partly because it housed industry, partly because the bombers came from the east, and if they hadn't found their target, they emptied their bombracks on the way home. The City is next door.

"But St. Paul's was never hit," Nigel continued. "And if I have one vision of England, it is of St. Paul's, big and black, still standing against the wall of flames that engulfed the East End one night. I believe the date was Dec. 29, 1940. I was 10 years old. They say the bombs bounced right off the roof." He turned to me. "England's history is one of recovering from disasters. The Blitz. Or look how we celebrate Dunkirk, a retreat. And, of course, the Fire. In fact, it started right over there, by the Monument." He pointed down William Street to the London Bridge. "In a little bakery on Pudding Lane. Imagine, coming right on the heels of the Plague."

At the height of the Plague in 1665, 6,000 people died in London a week. When a household became infected, the authorities sealed it up and posted a watchman to prevent escape. People lit vast bonfires in the streets, believing this would halt the disease.

A year later, in 1666, the Great Fire consumed four-fifths of the City in four days, destroying the medieval section. Christopher Wren, surveyor to Charles II, took it upon himself to rebuild. For two years, the authorities delayed his plans. By then, buildings had sprung up everywhere; they were made of brick, according to Charles' proclamation, the reason for all the brick you see today. As a result, Wren could not pursue his plan of a centralized city.

Ultimately, though, Wren built 51 churches, including his masterpiece, St. Paul's, on the site of the old church, where John Donne had been dean. Several early designs were rejected by the church, which wanted a Puritan-style hall. Wren finally began construction of a domed church in the shape of a cross on the king's authority alone. Today, mustached guardsmen chat with angels in the monuments inside, a uniquely English idea. Wren is buried in the church. His son's inscription at the tomb reads, "*Lector, si monumentum requiris circumspice*" ("Reader, if you require a monument, look about you").

Nigel mentioned one other fact about the City. Workers digging foundations recently discovered a temple to the ancient Babylonian god Mithras built by the Romans in the second century (near the corner of Victoria and Waitling streets). Interesting to think how international the ancient world really was, how even the oldest things in Europe sit on a past that stretches back to the Middle East and beyond.

We had passed the giant, windowless **Bank of England,** *Threadneedle Street* (which is closed to the public), and the **Royal Exchange,** *Poultry and Threadneedle streets* (which houses an insurance company and is open to public 11:30 a.m. to 2:30 p.m.). (Like many City streets, Poultry and Threadneedle were named for ancient trades.) Another landmark is the **Guildhall,** once a place of execution (of Charles II), now the site of dingy offices. Alas, we had another journey in mind.

The Guildhall in the City.

We continued on to Tower Hill and the famous **Tower of London.** Built by William the Conqueror from 1077 to 1097, and subsequently enlarged, the Tower of London was erected to keep the conquered people from revolting. It has served as a prison for many famous troublemakers. Sir Walter Raleigh spent 12 years here, and other prisoners have included Sir Thomas More, Thomas à Becket, and Anne Boleyn. The tower became an execution ground for many. (Anne Boleyn, suffering from a fear of axes, won execution by sword.) And here Richard III, the Hunchback, supposedly murdered his nephews.

"The Hunchback," said Nigel, referring to Richard. "An interesting philosophy, his. Quoth he, 'Conscience is but a word that cowards use, devised at first to keep the strong in awe. Our strongarms be our conscience, swords our law. March on, join bravely, let us to it pell-mell. If not to heaven, then hand in hand to hell.'"

"A good thought for the the trip before us," I replied.

The Tower of London was also briefly used as a bank, until Charles I decided to borrow the commoners' deposits. It now houses the Crown Jewels, a popular sight. But neither was this our destination.

We got out near the Tower Hill tube stop. I paused to look out at the Tower Bridge, which has sold many a postcard. (You can walk across the top for £2, *tel. 407-0922.*) Then we turned and walked across the street to the escalator up to the Docklands Light Railway.

* * *

I suppose I must interrupt my trip to the Docklands to tell you more about sightseeing in London. If you are going to be a tourist, you might as well do it properly. Following are the sights you really shouldn't miss.

London's must-sees

Art galleries

• **Courtauld Institute Galleries,** *Woburn Square, at the corner of Turrington Place; tel. 580-1015.*

The Courtauld contains the most important collection in Britain of impressionist and post-impressionist paintings. High points include a Van Gogh self-portrait *sans* ear and Manet's *Bar aux Folies Bergère*. Formerly located in Bloomsbury, the Courtauld also has works by Roger Fry and other Bloomsbury painters.

• **Institute of Contemporary Arts,** *the Mall; tel. 930-3647.*

The institute sponsors art shows, movies, plays, and other art happenings. The atmosphere is quite international and up-to-the-moment.

• **National Gallery,** *Trafalgar Square; tel. 839-3321.*

Situated at London's center, the National Gallery houses a great variety of paintings, although it is not nearly as large as the Louvre or New York's Metropolitan. The collection is strong in works from the Italian Renaissance and goes as far as post-impressionism.

• **National Portrait Gallery,** *St. Martin's Place, Trafalgar Square; tel. 930-1552, in the back of the National Gallery.*

The National Portrait Gallery houses some good art, but it is most notable for the famous English people displayed. You can tell a lot from the faces here—the family resemblances through generations are fascinating.

• **South Banks Arts Complex,** *Waterloo Bridge; tel. 928-3144.*

This complex houses the Hayward (an art gallery that specializes in contemporary art), the National Film Institute, the Museum of the Moving Image (see "Museums"), a theater, a music hall, several bookstores, pubs, and restaurants. Definitely worth seeing.

• **Tate Gallery,** *Millbank; tel. 821-1313.*

Mostly British, the Tate Gallery houses a good selection of works by Hogarth, Blake, Gainsborough, and Laurence, not to mention three floors by Turner. In addition, Beardsley, Rosetti, and Henry Moore are well-represented. Also displayed are a few works by Monet, Dègas, and Van Gogh, as well as some pieces by postwar Americans (such as Warhol and Lichtenstein).

• **Wallace Collection,** *Manchester Square; tel. 935-0687.*

Bequeathed by Sir Richard Wallace's widow, this museum houses 18th-century French art, along with period furniture and porcelain.

Churches

• **St. Bartholomew-the-Great,** *West Smithfield; tel. 606-1575.*

This is the second-oldest church in London after St. John's Chapel in the Tower. Begun in 1123 under Henry I, it was largely destroyed during the Reformation, but later rebuilt.

• **St. James's,** *Piccadilly.*

St. James's was built by Christopher Wren and restored after World War II. Its proximity to St. James's Palace made it a favorite of noblemen. Today, sermons and music are offered at lunchtime.

• **St. Martin-in-the-Fields,** *Trafalgar Square.*

St. Martin-in-the-Fields was built by Christopher Wren's pupil James Gibbs in 1726 on the site of a 13th-century church. Today, it is the church of the theater, where actors are memorialized. And it runs an outstanding program for the homeless. Concerts are held here at lunchtime.

• **St. Paul's Cathedral,** *St. Paul's Churchyard; tel. 248-2705.*

This church was architect Christopher Wren's masterpiece, built after the fire of 1666 on the site of an older church. Wren incorporated a dome into the design—against the wishes of church authorities, who wanted a Puritan-style hall. St. Paul's Cathedral survived almost undamaged the German Blitz during World War II.

• **Westminster Abbey,** *Parliament Square; tel. 222-5152.*

Part of Westminster Abbey was built in 1066 by Edward the Confessor. It is the most famous church in England, though not of the Church of England. It is a Royal Peculier, or a church belonging to the state.

• **Westminster Cathedral,** *Ashley Place.*

Westminster Cathedral is the premier Roman Catholic Church in London and the seat of the cardinal archbishop of Westminster. Finished in 1903, it is made primarily of brick.

Westminster Abbey, 1046.

Houses of the famous

• **Carlyle's House,** *24 Cheyne Row; tel. 352-7087.*

The great historian, known for his belief in heros, lived here from 1834 to 1881. The house is charming, preserved much as Carlyle left it.

• **Dickens' House,** *48 Doughty St.; tel. 405-2127.*

This was the author's home from 1837 to 1839. The prolific scribe penned *Oliver Twist, Nicholas Nickleby,* and parts of the *Pickwick Papers* during that period, and the house contains manuscripts, letters, and personal effects.

The blacking factory at Hungerford Stairs, where Dickens worked as a boy

• **Keats' House,** *Wentworth Place, Keats Grove; tel. 435-2062.*

This was the young author's residence from 1818 to 1821, when he died at the age of 26 while visiting Rome. In 1819, a widow and her daughter, Fanny Brawne, moved in next door, and Keats and Fanny became engaged. Beneath a plum tree, one May morning in 1819, Keats heard a nightingale sing and wrote "Ode to a Nightingale." The tree later blew down in a storm, an example of the very intensity and passion (and cruelty) that Keats revered as nature's.

• **Dr. Johnson's House,** *Gough Square; tel. 353-3745.*

This house, with its well-lit garret, is where Dr. Samuel Johnson, assisted by scribes, created his dictionary. Dr. Johnson lived here 10 years, 8 of which were spent at his task. A copy of the dictionary, letters, and personal effects are displayed.

Landmarks

• **Bank of England,** *Threadneedle Street.*

This massive building, known as the Old Lady of Threadneedle Street, encompasses four acres. Closed to the public, it lacks even windows—protection against the mob. Chartered in 1694 to facilitate England's war with Louis XIV of France, the Bank of England remained outside government control until 1946. The building itself was completed in 1833. Note the pink-liveried doormen.

• **Inns of Court: Gray's Inn,** *Gray's Inn Road;* **Middle** and **Inner temples,** *Fleet Street;* and **Lincoln's Inn,** *Chancery Lane.*

London's four Inns of Court, located in different parts of the city, are fascinating institutions that date from when the clergy abandoned law to professionals during the reign of Edward I.

The English system of law has two kinds of lawyers: solicitors and barristers. Solicitors deal with the public but may not plead cases in court. The more prestigious barristers do not deal with the public but, dressed in wigs, plead cases in court. To be a barrister you must belong to one of the four Inns of Court. The inns educate students, admit them to practice as barristers, and serve occasionally as dining halls and office space. However, a movement is afoot to erase the distinction between the two classes of lawyers, much as the Big Bang in finance erased distinctions between brokers and dealers.

Gray's Inn, one of the smaller inns, counts Francis Bacon as an alumnus and dates from the 14th century. Middle and Inner temples in the Temple, an enclave with a small entrance off Fleet Street, also date from the 14th century. The Temple itself once belonged to the Knights Templars, an order founded during the Crusades in Jerusalem in 1119. In the gardens of the Inner Temple, York and Lancaster supposedly plucked the roses that signaled the beginning of the War of Roses. Lincoln's Inn dates from the 15th century and counts among its members Sir Thomas More, Disraeli, and Gladstone.

• **Monument,** *Monument Street, Fish Street Hill.*

Built 202 feet from the bakery on Pudding Lane where the Great Fire broke out in 1666, the Monument, shaped like a giant Doric column, commemorates that event and marks the people's recovery. Designed by Christopher Wren, it was his first project following the Fire. From the top of its 311 steps, you have a fine view of London.

• **Old Bailey,** *Newgate Street.*

Old Bailey has been the scene of many a drama. It occupies the site of a former prison, in front of which executions took place. Spectators still crowd the courtroom for spectacular trials. Inquire at the Newgate Street entrance. Court is in session from 10 a.m. to 1 p.m. and from 2 p.m. to 4 p.m. daily.

• **Parliament** (also known as the Palace of Westminster, which formerly occupied the site).

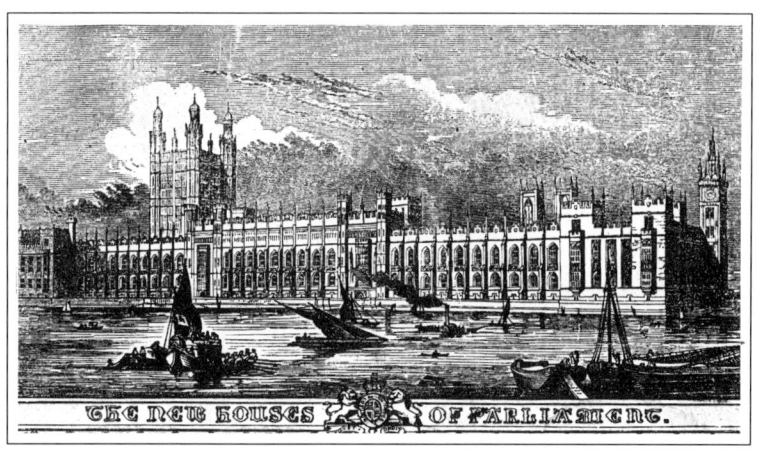

The new houses of Parliament.

A palace until 1529, when Henry VIII acquired Whitehall, this site became host to Parliament in 1547. The Commons sat in St. Stephen's Chapel, one of the few parts to survive the Fire of 1512 and later the Fire of 1834. The original Lords Hall has since perished. After the Fire of 1834, Barry designed a classic replacement, and his rival Pugin decked it out in its familiar Tudor trappings. Big Ben, actually a bell, fills the clock tower, while the palace's Victoria Tower contains a copy of every Parliamentary Act since 1497.

The reconstructed Lords Hall still holds daily court to democracy, and viewers with passes or who queue after 4:45 p.m for the Strangers Gallery may see the speeches and hooting in person. Each day some member of the government must endure a question-and-answer session beginning at 2 p.m., and the prime minister herself appears Tuesday and Thursday at 3:15 p.m. A light in the clock tower at night means the Commons is in session.

• **Royal Albert Hall** and **Albert Memorial,** *Kensington Gore; tel. 589-8212* or *589-9465.*

The Royal Albert Hall.

The round, glass-domed Albert Hall, conceived by Albert, was realized by Queen Victoria in memory of her consort. For years, it was known for its poor acoustics, but these have been improved. Every summer, the hall plays host to the Proms, London's premier music event.

Across the street from the Albert Hall, Victoria built another memorial, a comparatively humble statue of Albert set beneath an elaborately decorated canopy that looks like a missile about to take off.

• **Tower of London,** *Tower Hill; tel. 709-0765.*

The Tower of London was built by William the Conqueror in 1078 to keep the conquered in line. Originally, it consisted of a ring of walls, topped with 13 towers, but successive monarchs enlarged it. The tower has been besieged many times, but never taken. It served as a prison (for Thomas à Becket, Sir Thomas More, Sir Walter Raleigh, Anne Boleyn, King James I, and Queen Elizabeth) and as a place of execution. Richard III supposedly murdered two princes here. As recently as World War II, Rudolph Hess was held here, and assorted spies were shot in the tower.

The Tower of London is also home to the Crown Jewels, notably the Cullinan Diamond. The world's largest diamond, the Cullinan was mailed third class from South Africa, considered the safest way to get it to London.

Whitehall.

The tower is also the site of London's oldest church, the Chapel of St. John, built in 1080.

- **Whitehall.**

Once a palace, Whitehall (which runs from Parliament to Trafalgar) now refers to the motley collection of government buildings that surround Whitehall Street. The unattractive palace burned down in 1698 to the relief of almost everyone. The buildings here today are more important for what goes on inside them than for their architecture.

Museums

- **British Library and Museum,** *Great Russell Street; tel. 636-1555.*

The British Library was founded in 1753 on the basis of a bequest from Sir Hans Sloane. The libraries of George II and George III enlarged the collection. Since 1823, the library has received a copy of every book printed—a mile of new books per year.

The museum here charts the rise and fall of numerous civilizations, including Egypt, Assyria, Greece, Crete, Babylon, Nineveh, and Europe. It contains countless treasures of antiquity, including mummies from Egypt, the Elgin Marbles from Athens, and many rare books, notably the Magna Carta, the only copy of *Beowulf,* and illuminated manuscripts. The library is open to scholars only (who have included Karl Marx).

- **Geological Museum,** *Exhibition Road; tel. 589-3444.*

In addition to explanations of the geological formations in England, the Geological Museum boasts a strong collection of crystals.

• **Imperial War Museum,** *Lambeth Road; tel. 735-8922.*

Situated on the site of the old Bethlehem Hospital (the source of the word *bedlam*), the Imperial War Museum contains war gear and weapons, as well as famous documents, including Hitler's "Political Testament," dictated in his chancellery bunker while Goebbels and Bormann looked on.

• **London Toy and Model Museum,** *21-23 Craven Hill; tel. 262-7905* or *262-9450.*

A museum for children of all ages.

• **London Transport Museum,** *Covent Garden; tel. 379-6344.*

This museum tells the story of London transport, including the histories of the double-decker bus and the tube.

• **Madame Tussaud's,** *Marylebone; tel. 935-6861.*

Madame Tussaud began her museum in Paris, but revolutionary events drove her to London in 1802. The Chamber of Horrors may be the most interesting section, but rock stars and politicians are just as well-presented.

• **Museum of London,** *London Wall; tel. 600-3699.*

The Museum of London is devoted to the history of London from the Stone Age to the present. Excellent exhibits and dramatizations portray such milestones as the Plague, the Fire, and the Blitz.

• **Museum of Mankind,** *6 Burlington Gardens; tel. 437-2224.*

Formerly part of the British Museum, the Museum of Mankind traces human ethnography from ancient times to modern. Exhibits portray village life in far-flung parts of the world, notably Africa, South America, and the Pacific.

• **Museum of the Moving Image,** *South Banks Art Complex.*

This is London's newest and perhaps most fascinating museum. With movie sets as the background, you are given the opportunity to edit a Chaplin film, to read the news, or to follow a script from an autocue—all while interacting with circulating actors and actresses playing various roles. Don't miss this one.

• **Natural History Museum,** *Cromwell Road; tel. 589-6323.*

The Natural History Museum houses 40-million specimens of life, from the creepiest and crawliest insects to the clumsiest, most good-natured dinosaurs.

• **Science Museum,** *Exhibition Road; tel. 589-3456.*

This fun museum is big on old-fashioned machines as well as space-age exhibits. Don't visit on a weekday, when large numbers of schoolchildren take over the place.

• **John Soane Museum,** *13 Lincoln's Inn Fields; tel. 405-2107.*

The famous architect also collected art and drawings. His sensibility comes across in his innovative use of mirrors. In the basement is the sarcophagus of Seti I, king of Egypt in 1370 B.C.

• **Theatre Museum,** *Russell Street, Covent Garden; tel. 836-7891.*

London's theater tradition is second to none, and this museum does it justice. Examine props, costumes, and other memorabilia.

• **Victoria and Albert Museum,** *Cromwell Road; tel. 589-6371.*

This is a museum that an eccentric Victorian might have concocted. Lacking a central theme, exhibits are here because they are charming, not because they are in any way related. You can see anything from art to science to history. Look in at the period rooms and at Tippoo's Tiger, dating from 1808, a life-size model of a tiger devouring a white man.

Palaces

• **Buckingham Palace,** *the Mall.*

The public may not enter any part of the queen's residence, built by John Nash in 1830. When she is home, the flag flies aloft. The front of the palace is the site of the changing of the guard every morning at 11:30 a.m. The finest views are the queen's alone, facing back over 40 acres of land.

• **Kensington Palace,** *the Broad Walk, Kensington Gardens.*

Kensington Palace was a second home of kings from 1689 to 1760. Originally a stately house, William III, an asthma sufferer, bought it to escape the Thames by Whitehall Palace. He enlisted Christopher Wren to improve it, and the palace later served as childhood home to Queen Victoria. Most recently it is home to Prince Charles and Princess Di.

Buckingham Palace.

- **Lambeth Palace,** *Lambeth Road.*

This is the official residence of the archbishop of Canterbury. A few sections date from the 13th century, but most of the palace was built several centuries later. Its location on the river facilitated communication and transport.

- **St. James's Palace,** *Pall Mall.*

St. James's Palace was built by Henry VIII on the site of a former leper hospital. Of the original structure, only the tower and gatehouse remain, but additions now house the duke and duchess of Kent. Not long after Henry built the palace, he decided to take over Cardinal Wolsey's palace in Hampton Court instead (his former housemate Anne Boleyn's head having meanwhile fallen by the wayside). Not until Whitehall Palace burned down in 1698, did this became the official residence of the sovereign. In 1837, the court moved to Buckingham. Nevertheless, ambassadors remain accredited to the court of St. James. The palace is closed to the public, though the Chapel Royal, built in 1532, is open for Sunday services in winter.

Parks

Many would argue that London has the worlds' finest parks, complete with chaises lounges where you can rest your feet (some require a ticket), birds, flowers, and, of course, acres and acres of green (thanks to the climate). While almost all are safe during the day, it is not a good idea to wander through them alone at night.

- **Hampstead Heath,** *north of London.*

This is less a park than an area of unspoiled land that includes woods, grassy areas, and ponds. Once a haven for highwaymen, later a favorite among artists, today Hampstead Heath entertains people looking for a place to relax. Women may swim at Kenwood Ladies' Pond, men at Highgate Men's Pond, and both at the Mixed Bathing Pond.

Nearby is the Kenwood House facing Hampstead Lane, a charming 18th-century estate. Down Hampstead Lane (or, from the southeast tip of the part, via Swain's Lane), is Highgate Cemetery. Karl Marx and George Eliot are buried in the eastern half of the cemetery, but the western part has a macabre charm all its own. The Friends of Highgate Cemetery, who fought to reopen the site, now donate their time to give tours, an outstanding example of English eccentricity. Note the sign warning, "Don't feed the rats."

- **Hyde Park** and **Kensington Gardens,** *at the center of London.*

These gardens comprise a whopping 630 acres. Originally part of Westminster Abbey, they became a deer park under Henry VIII and later a people park. The corner at Marble Arch on the Mayfair side is known as Speakers' Corner. Here each Sunday soapbox speakers harangue the crowds on religion, politics, and simple lunacy. Some of the speakers are quite gifted, as are some of the hecklers.

Moving west is the Serpentine, a long, meandering body of water where you can swim and boat. (A somewhat dirty café in the middle serves food and beverages.) At the south side of the park, facing the Royal Albert Hall, is the Albert Memorial and a horse track, Rotten Row (derived from Route du Roi). The western side of the park formerly comprised the grounds of Kensington Palace (hence its name, Kensington Gardens).

The Crystal Palace in Hyde Park.

- **Regent's Park,** *tel. 722-3333.*

London's largest park is the site of the London Zoo. This extensive zoo, founded in 1826, includes Lord Snowdon's aviary, which is gigantic and worth seeing. Don't miss the chimpanzees' tea party each afternoon. The park also includes lakes and promenades, Queen Mary's Gardens, and the Regent's Park Canal. Its wide-open spaces make it a popular place for cricket and soccer matches (and even American expatriate softball games). The Open Air Theater hosts performances in the summer.

- **St. George's Gardens,** *Mayfair.*

This is one of the prettiest parks in all London. St. George's Church and ivy-covered buildings create a fine background for this beautiful pause in the city.

- **St. James's Park,** *across the Mall from St. James's Palace.*

This is a pleasant place to promenade or just to sit and relax. Designed by Nash to emulate the country gardens of Kent and Sussex, it was originally a marsh. Henry VIII had the land drained to make a deer park. Wandering through the park today are swans, ducks, and even flamingoes.

- **Victoria Tower Gardens,** *Millbank, south of Parliament.*

These gardens offer a view of Parliament and the mighty tree-lined Thames. Free chairs and a Rodin sculpture (*The Burghers of Calais*) add to the charm.

Regions of interest

- **Bloomsbury.**

No longer a hotbed of avant-garde activity, as in the days of Virginia Woolf, Bloomsbury has settled into a quiet, leafy calm. Home to the British Museum and London University, it has a decidedly scholarly cast and is popular among tourists. Its proximity to the City makes it a favorite place to have a drink in the evening. Still, with its many small parks, it retains a quiet, unhurried feel.

- **Chelsea.**

This region lies slightly south of Kensington along the river. Its central artery, King's Road, was once a royal road to Hampton Court and beloved by bandits. In the 19th century, it became home to well-heeled artists and writers (such as Wilde, Carlyle, and Whistler), and in the 1960s, it underwent a renaissance after Mary Quant opened a shop here selling her miniskirts.

For a while King's Road served as the main drag for first hippies, then punk rockers (Sex Pistols manager Malcolm McLaren has a shop here). However, today the area is too expensive for anyone that rough around the edges, but people still flock to King's Road, especially on Sunday, to strut their stuff. Near the river you may see people in red-coated costumes. They are retired soldiers, pensioners from the Chelsea Royal Hospital. (Until recently, it was a hanging offense to impersonate a pensioner.)

- **The City.**

Located around the original one-square-mile walled Roman city of Londinium, the City is the oldest part of London. Every year, the City's livery companies (or guilds) select a lord mayor from the City's aldermen and sheriffs. And every year, the lord mayor, dressed in full regalia, makes his traditional procession through the City. If you look closely at the badges of police patrolling the City, you'll notice they're different from those of other bobbies. Since the Magna Carta, every king has granted sovereignty to the City. He does not enter without permission from the lord mayor.

The City is synonymous with finance. Every day, two-million commuters pour in, only to depart again come evening, leaving lonely, deserted streets at night. Almost all of the City was destroyed in the Great Fire of 1666, but the rebuilding left it with many churches designed by Christopher Wren, of which St. Paul's is the greatest.

Half the City's residents live in the Barbican, a fortress-like development that features co-ops, council flats (project apartments), stores, and a theater.

Many City streets are named for wares once sold on them (Threadneedle and Poultry, for example), but most of the business now is in stocks, bonds, and insurance.

- **Covent Garden.**

Designed by Inigo Jones, Covent Garden has had a rich and ribald history. Following the suppression of theater and night life on the South Bank, it became London's theater center, and many theaters remain, especially on Drury Lane. A market dominated the central square until 1973, when rats and overcrowding forced it to move south of the river. In 1980, the cobblestoned square was redeveloped, and today it houses a pleasant shopping mall that is a good place to enjoy home-grown street entertainment.

- **Fleet Street.**

Fleet Street, which occupies the historic road from the City to

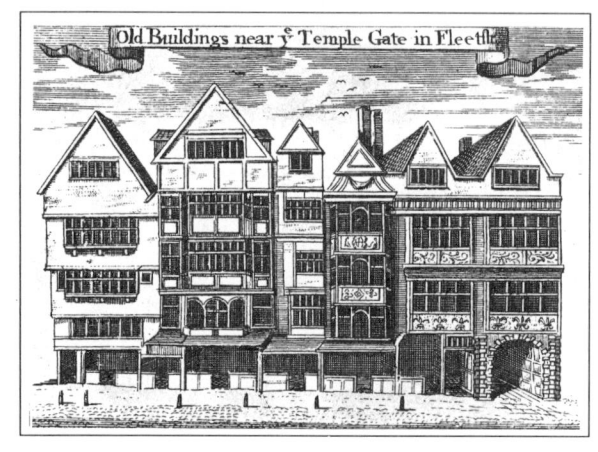

Fleet Street of yore.

Westminster, has long been synonymous with newspapers in England. However, the law courts, including Old Bailey, dominate one end of the street, and the newspapers are rapidly deserting the other for cheaper rents in the Docklands. Nevertheless, Fleet Street will surely endure as a synonym for some of the best and worst in journalism.

Needless to say, this area has had a colorful history. The Temple Bar, a simple spike in the middle of the road, marks the former gates of the City, where traitors' heads were deposited.

Two-tiered Tower Bridge is immediately recognizable. A one-of-a-kind innovation, it permitted people to walk across the top while tall-masted ships plied the river below.

- **Hampstead.**

Once a colony of artists, Hampstead today is filled with twee (cute) little shops, but it retains the pleasant atmosphere of a village. While the artists and intellectuals have gone, the expression "boys from Hampstead" still is used in newspapers to refer to leftists (that is, the Oxbridge-educated intelligentsia).

- **Kensington.**

This area, officially a royal borough, runs south of Hyde Park from Sloane Street out to Earl's Court. Originally roamed by outlaws who gave travelers from Westminster to Hampton Court occasional alarm, it is now one of the best (and most expensive) addresses in London. Recently it became known as Sloane Ranger Heaven (thanks in part to former resident Lady Di). Technically, Lady Di remains a resident at nearby Kensington Palace in the park. Kensington continues beyond Kensington Gardens, but becomes less fashionable north of Bayswater Road.

- **The Mall.**

    The Mall was created in 1906 to give London a proper place to hold processions (it's comparable to Paris' Champs-Elysées). The Mall runs between St. James's-the-park and St. James's-the-neighborhood, from Trafalgar to Buckingham Palace.

- **Mayfair.**

    Mayfair lies above Piccadilly but below Oxford Street, between Park Lane to the west and Regent Street to the east. It is the site of some of London's best shops (New Bond Street), tailors (Savile Row), and hotels (Brown's, Claridge's, and the Connaught). Here you will also find the American embassy (Grosvenor Square) and some of the city's most expensive real estate. Many of Mayfair's streets, such as Brook, Carlos Place, South Audley, and Curzon, calm and pleasant, are synonymous with London elegance.

- **Piccadilly** (neither street nor road—it needs no further appellation).

    Piccadilly runs approximately parallel to the Mall from Piccadilly Circus to Hyde Park Corner. It divides St. James's from Mayfair and is famous for its elegant stores (and the Royal Academy of Art).

Piccadilly about 1775.

- **Soho.**

    Founded by Huguenots after the Revocation of the Edict of Nantes, Soho has been a traditional mecca for foreigners. Perhaps for that reason, it has traditionally been associated with foreign restaurants, the theater, and sex. A recent crackdown has cleared the area of most visible evidence of the latter. Fortunately, the theaters and restaurants remain (Greek and Frith streets are especially famous for their restaurants).

Soho became a theater capital after Shaftesbury Avenue was cut through the slums at the beginning of the century. Wardour Street, London's film district, is in Soho, and recently many young designers opened boutiques in the area.

• **Trafalgar Square,** *Whitehall.*

The de facto center of London, Trafalgar Square is known for Admiral Nelson's statue, its fountain, pigeons, and the looming presence of the National Gallery. London's official center (for figuring mileage) is located in the forecourt of nearby Charing Cross Station.

Trafalgar Square.

Chapter VI

The Docklands Light Railway is pleasant. But nothing prepared me for the breadth, the wonder, and the scale of the development of the Docklands. Clearly, this is London's future, for good or bad. It is a bold enterprise, in which conscience is playing little part, and it is fitting that it should take place at the source of England's power: London's miles of docks.

Abandoned when union workers chose not to work at all rather than take drastic cuts in wages, the London docks have a rich history. Street names are reminiscent of the days when wooden vessels were loaded and unloaded by hand: Morocco Street, the East India Docks—all conjure up the smells and tastes of commodities, such as tea, coffee, and animal hides, which today reach London in sealed containers from Southampton.

The Docklands are now nothing more than one giant construction site, and there is little reason to get off the railway. (If you'd like to visit the touristy but ancient Prospect of Whitby, a 600-year-old pub where diarist Samuel Pepys quenched his thirst, you're better off walking along the Thames from Tower Hill through St. Catherine's Dock.) Nevertheless, the prospects of the Docklands are amazing. Cranes literally fill the horizon. But as we rode through, I noticed that none of them were moving.

"They're all on their lunch break," laughed Nigel.

We got off at the end of the line and took the foot tunnel over to Greenwich. The foot tunnel, while not particularly pleasant, was a triumph of 19th-century engineering. It enabled South Bank residents to go to work on the docks and was an improvement on cross-river ferries. Walking through the tunnel, you can imagine the hordes of consumptive (tubercular), pipe-smoking characters who crowded the tunnel every morning, some carrying cakes to sell, others with canes, still others sporting tattoos and muscles. Today the tunnel is filled with screaming schoolchildren. The controversy over the Docklands is related in the graffiti on the walls of the tunnel: "Steam the Rich" and, alternatively, "Steam the Poor."

After a few minutes, we emerged in pleasant Greenwich. The first thing I noticed was the impressive *Cutty Sark,* the fastest clipper of her day, named from Robert Burns' poem "Tam O'Shanter."

A tour of Greenwich should include a stop at **Relcy Antiques,** *9 Nelson Road; tel. 852-2812,* where you can find fascinating nautical antiques, anything from a deep-sea diver's outfit to a carved mermaid. Also visit the antiques market (held only on weekends). Or spend your time in Greenwich visiting the area's excellent museums: the **National Maritime Museum** and the **Old Royal Observatory.** The place in Greenwich to eat is **Le Papillon,** *57 Greenwich Church St.; tel. 858-2668.*

The Cutty Sark *dominates the harbor at Greenwich.*

Nigel and I walked up to **St. Alfege's Church** to begin our Greenwich tour. A run-down, poor church, with limestone gravestones that have worn away over time, it conveys with remarkable poignancy life by the sea. Many of the tombs are of sailors. Behind the church is the Greenwich National School of Education and Industry of Girls Instituted MDCCCXIV (1814). I cringed at the word *industry.*

"Straight out of Dickens," said Nigel.

Walking through Greenwich, it's not difficult to imagine girls whose fathers had died at sea or who had been born of sailors in port. They got a quick education at the National School of Education and Industry in the ways of the world, then went to work at KWP Metals across the street. In those days, poverty was considered a moral failing. From the windows at the back of the school, you can imagine the girls looking out for a glimpse of green.

All the churches in Greenwich are topped with weather vanes.

"That east wind bodes no good," Nigel quoted from his vast store of stage lines. But would a west wind have boded better?

110

Considerably cheerier are the National Maritime Museum, which documents England's rise to naval prominence, and the Old Royal Observatory, at the top of a hill, where you can stand on the prime meridian, by which all the world's clocks are set. It fixes Greenwich Mean Time. Here Halley discovered his famous comet. And here is housed an amazing collection of clocks, including the one Lieutenant Bligh carried on the *Bounty* and the one Fletcher Christian took to Pitcairn Island. I struck up a conversation with one of the guards, who turned out to have been a sailor. That's one of the fascinating things about Greenwich—it's filled with old sailors.

"That really belonged to Captain Bligh?" I asked.

"He woz neveh a captain, neveh mor'n a lootnant," this good-natured man explained. He proceeded to give me quite an informative lecture on the subject, which he concluded with, "Yes, those were the days of hard men and wooden ships. Punishment for major crimes wuz 20 lashes from ivry officer on t' boat."

It turned out that the guard had been in the Royal Navy. Was it like that for him?

"No, no," he laughed. "But I can remember the days of pickin oakum for punishment." This involved breaking up tarry rope into shreds to caulk the boards. "They couldn't ave yeo jes sitting there. Naoh, they had to have yeo doin something. After awhile your fingers'd be bleedin."

"What would they put you in for?" I asked.

"Strikin an officer. Smooglin." We talked about life on board.

"In the ole days we did'n ave no cook. Not like today. No, they'd give us the food, see, and we'd have to cook it, whether it was soup we were makin or beef. An we'd ave to make our own Yorkshie puddin if we wuz gonna have one, and cook it all up ourselves. Not like today."

He described the "af ration of rum." At 11 each day sailors got their measures of rum. Some would drink their rations on the spot, others would hoard them for a drunk.

I asked him where he went when he got into port, say in London. Did he go to the West End, perhaps?

"Naow, we'd go right up wah we wuz. No sense wasting time, and the West End'd be too dear. If we docked in Greenwich, we'd walk up and find a place in Greenwich. If we docked on the uthuh side, on the Isle of Dogs, we'd go there. We just wanted to, you know, ave a few pints and chase after the girls."

I asked if any of the old pubs were still around.

"Well, there's some, but they're all chartered up, spiled, that's what I say." He mentioned the Cutty Sark Pub. It occurred to me that I might not have fit in in the old days.

I saw Nigel poke his head in the doorway. It was time to go, and I said goodbye to the noble sailor.

"It was a good life," he concluded, shaking his head. "I wouldn't a had it different."

"Amazing, your talking to that chap," said Nigel. "But then you're American. Being English, it's quite unlikely he and I would ever talk. Though we might want to, we're too far apart in class."

Greenwich is the site of the **Royal Naval College** (open from 2:30 p.m. to 5 p.m.; admission is free), where many naval officers have been educated and where Conrad set the beginning of his first novel, *Victory*. But Nigel and I didn't take time to visit. We boarded a boat down at the port and headed back upriver to Westminster. Yes, I saw a glimmer of what Engels had described, but the river had a slightly tired look. The sun was setting ahead of us, as though relaxing after all those years of carrying so many goods, so much commerce, so much history.

We dined at Nigel's club, the **Garrick,** *Garrick Street,* in Covent Garden, where Nigel introduced me to several famous actors, some of whom were performing at the club that night. The vibrations of the place were amazing. And amidst all the hubbub were the quaint touches that make a place special: paintings stacked to the ceiling, reading stands for gentlemen dining alone.

After dinner, we walked over to Charing Cross Road and saw *Hamlet* at the Phoenix, Noel Coward's old theater. The play starred talented Kenneth Branagh and his company. "There is more on heaven and earth, Horatio, than is dreamt of in your philosophy," says Hamlet early on. At the end of the play, bodies strewn on the stage, I felt a post-tragedy catharsis and was ready to return to my hotel. I bid good night to Nigel, who went backstage to congratulate the performers.

Back at the Savoy, I sat down to record the day's experiences. But I couldn't keep Jenny Wilde from interrupting my thoughts. Where had she gone, I wondered? Finally, I got up to take a look at her bag. I noticed that the initials, J.W., were the same as mine. I remembered Jenny saying, "Don't let anyone have this bag." Methinks the lady doth protest too much, I thought. I poured myself a nightcap and took one last look at the play of lights over the river.

I was ready for sleep, but I had promised myself (not to mention my publisher) to write about theater in London. Telling myself that there's no time like the present (and drawing upon the inspiration from Nigel), I sat down to write.

* * *

A night out in London

Theater

London has the best theater in the world. Understand that, as a New Yorker, I wince when I say that. But the truth is, New York now imports most of its big hits from London.

What's more, theatergoing in London is cheaper than in New York. West End tickets cost one-half to three-quarters as much as Broadway tickets. And London's fringe performances are less expensive than off-Broadway productions.

During the postwar years (the days first of Olivier, Gielgud and

The Globe Theater.

113

Guinness, Maggie Smith, and Finney and Bates), London theater thrived on government subsidies. Now those are virtually gone, and artists complain that a mercenary spirit of mediocrity has seized the West End, as producers grow wary of risks. But good theater remains. And London still has two large subsidized theaters—the Royal Shakespeare Company and the National Theater—as well as about 40 West End or mainstream commercial theaters and 50 theaters known as fringe.

An evening at a London theater would not be complete without a drink—or two—during intermission. Order your drink from the bartender before the play begins, and between acts you will find your refreshment waiting (marked with your name); you can relax while others fight at the bar. Veteran theatergoers order a bottle of wine—or champagne—to share.

An alternative is to remain in the theater during the break and purchase an ice cream from one of the women who move gracefully among the aisles. Some theaters also serve sandwiches in a special area off the bar.

Obtaining tickets

Of course, the primary question when planning a night out at the theater is what to see. Generally, three or four "hot tickets" are playing in London. These plays are almost always worth seeing, but they're frequently sold out six months in advance. However, that doesn't mean you can't get tickets. Theaters sell only about one-third of the available tickets themselves, consigning the lion's share to agencies. (When buying tickets in London, you'll notice that they don't always look like the tickets you're accustomed to buying. Tickets from agencies look simply like slips of paper.)

The following reputable ticket agencies usually have tickets to even the hottest shows. (Be prepared to pay 15% to 20% over the actual ticket price. And don't expect to always be told the exact location of the seats you're buying.)

• **Exchange Travel,** *Theatre Museum, Covent Garden, Russell Street.*

• **First Call,** *tel. 240-7200* (100 lines).

First Call takes 24-hour credit-card bookings.

• **Keith Prowse & Company,** *Plantation House, Fenchurch Street; tel. 626-2784; 44 Shaftesbury Ave.; tel. 437-8976;* and *234 W. 44th St., New York, NY 10036; (212)398-1430.*

Messrs. Keith and Prowse hold claim to having invented the modern ticket. In 1780, they ran a musical instruments business. In those days, you paid for your theater tickets at the door, so clients would ask merchants to send a boy down to reserve them a place. The enterprising partners convinced theater owners to number seats, and they've dominated the business ever since.

Keith Prowse handles most big hotel concessions, including Brown's, Claridge's, Grosvenor House, Inn on the Park, the Inter-Continental, the Park Lane, the Savoy, and the Westbury. It also has outlets in Harrods, Selfridges, and the Virgin Megastore on Oxford Street.

• **Obtainables Ltd.,** *Panton House, 25 Haymarket; tel. 839-5363, 839-4416, or 839-4532.*

Virtually everything is available here—at a price.

• **Sidi,** *161 Drury Lane; tel. 831-7968,* and *Jubilee Market Road, opposite the New London Theatre; tel. 242-8748.*

When other agents fail, Sidi may have what you want.

• **Ticketmaster,** *tel. 379-4444.*

Ticketmaster takes 24-hour credit-card bookings (you must know exactly which seats you want before you call).

The box office

Another way to obtain tickets is to visit the theater box office, where you can pore over the seating chart and decide exactly what you want. Generally, you can pay with cash, check (in pounds), or credit card (a handful of theaters stop credit-card sales at 6:30 p.m., when their credit bureaus close).

Tickets by telephone and mail

You also can buy theater tickets over the phone, using a credit card. The telephone number for credit-card purchases is usually different from the regular number. Most theaters stipulate that you must pick up tickets reserved over the telephone within three days.

I've never done it, but some organized souls (those with filofaxes) write ahead for tickets—a sensible option for sold-out shows. Enclose a check or money order (in pounds) and a self-addressed envelope and provide an alternate date.

Tickets from touts

London does not have a well-developed scalping system. Touts, as they're known, work only the hottest shows and charge higher prices than agencies. What's worse, they sell fake tickets and generally prey on tourists. If you must buy from a tout, wait until right before curtain time and examine the ticket carefully before paying for it. Unfortunately, fake tickets often look like real ones.

Return tickets

What if the agencies and the theater box office are sold out of tickets for the show you want to see? A good way to obtain tickets for a sold-out show at the last minute is to take your place on the returns line. Holders of tickets are allowed to return them usually up to curtain time. In addition, people sometimes reserve tickets over the telephone and then are unable to show up to claim them. These tickets go on sale a few at a time beginning an hour or so before curtain. If you arrive a good hour early to any show but the *ne plus ultra,* you stand a reasonable chance of getting in.

While you're standing on the returns line, someone may approach you offering tickets purchased at an agency. Speak up quickly if you're interested. If you're willing to pay what the purchaser paid (marked on the tickets), he should be willing to sell them to you. You may be able to bargain the price down slightly, but be careful: Bargain too hard, and someone else will snatch the tickets away from you.

Cheap tickets

If you're not particular about what you see, head to the half-price booth in Leicester Square (on the Piccadilly side). Monday through Saturday from 2:30 p.m. to 6:30 p.m. (the booth opens at 12 p.m. for matinees), tickets are sold here for half-price (plus a £1 booking charge). Lines may be long in the summer.

In general, matinees and previews are less expensive than regular performances (though rarely as good). And, of course, a matinee may fit better into your schedule or allow you to see two shows in one day. At some theaters (marked with an "S" or an abbreviation of "Concessions" in the paper), students and old-age pensioners can buy cheap (£5) unsold tickets if they stand on line two hours before show time.

The National Theater Company sells unsold tickets plus a selection of choice seats in the first and second rows at huge discounts beginning at 10 a.m. on the day of a performance.

What to wear

Londoners dress nicely—but not formally—for the theater. Always wear light clothing. In summer, air conditioning may consist of a fan, and in winter, the heat is usually too high.

Where to sit

What we call orchestra seats, the British call the stalls. These are always good seats (although those in back lie in the shadow of the dress circle, or balcony). The stalls are best for shows with lots of trap doors, such as *The Phantom of the Opera*.

The dress circle reaches quite close to the stage. Seats toward the front of the dress circle usually cost as much as the best of the stalls and give an elevated perspective on the action (which I enjoy).

Andrew Lloyd Webber's The Phantom of the Opera *remains a crowd-pleaser.*

As you move upward, prices naturally go down. For a good play, however, I recommend sticking to the stalls, the dress circle, the boxes (as long as they're unobstructed), or, at the very least, the upper circle. Seats in the upper balcony of a large theater, called the gods, are far from a tiny stage, and the angle of the rise is Himalayan.

What to see

To find out what's good, pick up a copy of *Time Out* or *City Limits*. Both give capsule descriptions of running plays and review the newest productions. *Time Out* was first published in the 1960s as an alternative magazine. It has mellowed with age and today offers excellent coverage of the arts. *What's On,* the *Evening Standard,* and the *Guardian* also publish schedules and reviews of shows.

If all else fails, the theater provides some judge of the fare. For Shakespeare, you can't go wrong with the Royal Shakespeare Company (RSC), which in 1982 moved to the **Barbican Centre,** *tel. 628-2295* or *628-9760* for information, *628-8759* or *638-8891* for reservations; *tube: Barbican.* This outwardly inhospitable fortress (pedestrians must enter via the car park) set in the middle of nowhere (an unpleasant, 10-minute walk from the City) contains flats, council flats (or projects), shops, restaurants, and two theaters (the Barbican, home of the RSC, and the Pit, which specializes in the avant garde). Ironically, the Barbican covers famous Grub Street, where hack writers once plied their trade, composing sonnets, plays, dictionaries—anything for a pound.

Attendance at the RSC has gone down since it moved to the Barbican Centre, but not because of the theater itself. The balconies lean forward, ensuring that no seat is more than 65 feet from the stage (however, the lack of aisles makes reaching the balconies a bit awkward). The Pit provides pit-like intimacy for fringe productions.

The **Old Vic,** *across from Waterloo Station on the South Bank; tel. 928-7616* or *261-1821* for credit-card bookings; *tube: Waterloo,* is probably your best bet for innovative stagings of the classics. The Old Vic (once a nickname, this title is now official) was the home of the National Theater Company for much of this century. I saw some fine theater here in my youth. Now owned by Honest Ed Mervish, the Old Vic maintains the highest standards of theater.

A few yards away, a former butcher's shop houses the **Young Vic,** *tel. 928-6363* or *379-6433* for credit-card bookings, known for its repertory productions, some specifically for young people. Ticket prices are low (£7.50, £3.50 for students), and the quality is high. This is a good place to take the children.

In 1976 the National Theater Company moved to the **South Bank Arts Complex,** *tube: Waterloo* (walk toward the river from the station; the entrance is on river side). This futuristic complex—better designed than the Barbican—contains three theaters: the Olivier, the Lyttleton, and the Cottesloe. (You can reach the box office for all three theaters by calling *928-2252* or *928-8126.* For information between 10 a.m. and 11 p.m., you also can call *633-0880.*) The Olivier (named for Laurence, its first director) is used for large productions; the Lyttleton is traditional; and the Cottesloe, modeled on the Elizabethan Inn Yards, was designed for experimental works. For repertory, you can't do better.

In addition to the three theaters, the South Bank Arts Complex also houses an art gallery, restaurants, and bookstores. The convenient **Orations Restaurant,** *tel. 928-2033, extension 531* during the day and *561* in the evening, takes orders until 11 p.m.

In the 1950s and 1960s, the **Royal Court Theater,** *Sloane Square; tube: Sloane Square,* was the place to see cutting-edge theater (including John Osborne's famous *Look Back in Anger,* an attack on postwar English

Leicester Square in 1754.

society). The Royal Court is known today as a theatergoer's theater, revered by theater-lovers for its nourishment of young talent. The Royal Court's English Stage Company concentrates on new plays—although all are not as successful as Osborne's project.

Balcony seats in this small, somewhat run-down theater are cheap but closer than usual (experimental stagings may favor the stalls). By joining a club sponsored by the Royal Court, you can see plays at reduced rates year-round (ask for information at the box office). And ticket prices are sometimes reduced on Monday. Upstairs is a small fringe theater.

Outdoor theater

From June through September, the New Shakespeare Company makes Regent's Park its home. Weather permitting, there are few nicer ways to spend a summer night than watching Shakespeare (or any other of the classics) in the midst of your own midsummer night's dream as the sun sets over the trees. Early arrivers get the seats nearest the stage—farther back you may find it difficult to hear. Bring a blanket, wine, and victuals (although decent food and drink is on sale; blankets also can be hired).

Tickets to these outdoor performances cost from £4 to £10. To reserve tickets, call *486-2431* (*379-6433* for credit-card bookings) between 10 a.m. and 6 p.m. (It is a good idea to call for reservations, because seating is limited.)

The **Holland Park Open Air Theater,** *tel. 933-2542, extension 52; tube: Kensington High Street,* offers a more intimate, almost Renaissance atmosphere. From June to August, Tuesday through Sunday, theater and opera performances are alternatively staged. Music is free on Sunday at 3 p.m.

Fringe theater

I can make no guarantees about fringe theater. From night to night, you never know what you'll see. But lovers of theater appreciate the sheer piquancy of fringe. Here ideas germinate and ferment, then ultimately bubble forth into the mainstream—perhaps into a West End hit. Moreover, prices are generally low, and shows are rarely sold out.

Tickets to most fringe shows can be purchased at the **Fringe Box Office,** located in the foyer of the **Duke of York's Theatre,** *St. Martin's Lane, in the heart of the West End; tel. 379-6002* (the box office is open Monday through Thursday from 10 a.m. to 6 p.m.; Friday and Saturday from 10 a.m. to 5 p.m.).

Fringe shows are listed and reviewed in *Time Out* and *City Limits.*

Better-known venues are listed below.

- **Bush Theatre,** *Bush Hotel, Shepherds Bush Green; tel. 743-3388; tube: Goldhawk Road.*

Located above the pub of the Bush Hotel, the Bush Theatre is an important venue for young playwrights.

- **Donmar Warehouse,** *41 Earlham St.; tel. 240-8230; tube: Covent Garden.*

Used by the RSC as an experimental workshop a few years ago, the Donmar has brought much new talent to the fore. Theater in the evenings gives way to cabaret late at night, featuring performances, readings, and monologues.

- **Institute of Contemporary Arts Theatre,** *Nash House, Carlton Terrace, the Mall; tel. 930-3647; tube: Charing Cross.*

Only a stone's throw from Trafalgar and across the Mall from St. James's Park, the Institute of Contemporary Arts is as much a movement as a theater. Its facilities include an art gallery, a bookstore, a cinema, and a café. David Bowie assists in the fund raising for the institute, which specializes in political and social works, including works by women. Plays performed here are always provocative.

- **Mermaid Theatre,** *Puddle Dock, Blackfriars; tel. 236-5568* or *236-5568* for credit-card bookings; *tube: Blackfriars.*

Pure but adventurous drama is the hallmark of the Mermaid. New works alternate with classic revivals, and all are well-produced.

While the theater is one of the greatest things about London, the city offers many other ways to spend an evening.

Opera

The magnificent **Royal Opera House,** *Covent Garden, Bow and Floral streets; tel. 240-1066, 240-1911, 240-9815,* or *836-6093,* hosts London opera companies and international stars performing classics in the original language. Tickets cost as much as £40. The **English National Opera** (ENO) at the **London Coliseum,** *St. Martin's Lane; tel. 836-3161* or *240-5258* for credit-card bookings, performs the same works in English. Tickets cost as much as £22.50.

Currently, a battle rages between the two. Critics lambast the Royal Opera House for its stuffiness, while praising ENO's innovative stagings. What's more, the Royal Opera has come under attack for its plans to erect an office block in the middle of Covent Garden.

Nonetheless, no one will ever convince me that *La Boheme* or *Tosca* or *Carmen* sounds better in translation. Despite the Royal Opera's scandalous subtitling of non-Italian works on a hideous display above the stage, I must cast my vote with the Royalists.

Stand-by tickets (which cost only £12.50) go on sale one hour before curtain. And some mornings, the guard at the Floral Street entrance hands out free passes to aficionados for the 10:30 a.m. rehearsals.

For less weighty fare, head to the **Sadler's Wells Theatre,** *Rosebery Avenue; tel. 278-8916; tube: Angel,* not far from Camden Passage. Here the Sadler's Wells Opera Company stages operettas—more to the point, it stages the works of Gilbert and Sullivan.

Ballet

Until recently, the Sadler's Wells Theatre was also the home of the Sadler's Wells Royal Ballet. However, that company, rechristened the Royal Opera Ballet, now performs principally at the Royal Opera House. Tickets cost up to £45.65. (Rear amphitheater seats are held and sold at 10 a.m. on the day of a performance. Queues form early, and it's one ticket per person.) The Sadler's Wells Theatre now plays host to leading visiting companies, English as well as foreign. (Mercifully, in the case of ballet, language is not an issue.)

The London Coliseum is the home of the Festival Ballet.

Film

Cinema-lovers will find much to engage them in London. Again, *Time Out* and *City Limits* run thorough listings of what's showing. In addition to the latest hits at Leicester Square, you may wish to take advantage of the city's excellent repertory. You're likely to see films here, both British and American, that aren't shown in the United States. London's primary cinemas are listed below.

• **Curzon,** *Curzon Street; tel. 499-3737.*

This is the place to see first-run art films. It is an uncommonly comfortable cinema.

• **Everyman Cinema,** *Hollybush Vale, Hampstead; tel. 435-1525; tube: Hampstead.*

The Everyman has a thematic repertory—Marlon Brando one day, screwball comedy the next. A yearly membership is £1; tickets are £3.

• **Institute of Contemporary Art,** *Nash House, Carlton Terrace, the Mall; tel. 930-3647; tube: Charing Cross.*

Little-known films, many by independent film makers, are shown here. Tickets are £3 (half-price tickets are available on Monday).

• **National Film Theatre,** *South Bank Arts Complex; tel. 928-3232* or *437-4355* for membership information; *tube: Waterloo* or *Embankment.*

Members only may see films here. A one-week membership is 70p; tickets are £3. Cinema fanatics will enjoy this theater's 11-day film viewings (up to 6 different films).

• **Roxie Cinema Club,** *76 Wardour St.; tel. 439-3657; tube: Piccadilly* or *Leicester Square.*

The Roxie is the cinema-lover's bread and butter. Its double features are changed daily. Tickets are £3.

Chapter VII

I checked out of the Savoy and into Claridge's the following day. If the Savoy was founded on show business, Claridge's is a preserve for royalty, a place for people with responsibilities. Since its founding, Claridge's has never permitted dancing or entertainment in its ballrooms—however, it has hosted many tasteful coming-out balls for debutantes (which are strictly policed).

I wanted peace and quiet. My suite at Claridge's looked out on the buildings opposite. Gone was the marvelous view at the Savoy, but there are other things in life. Kings have camped out at Claridge's, I thought; I ought to be able to manage.

Anyway, I was more preoccupied with thoughts of Jenny than with the details of my accommodations.

It was a sunny Sunday afternoon when I made my way to the boathouse to meet her. En route, I made a detour to buy some flowers at the colorful Berwick Street market. I passed stalls selling vegetables, fruit, clothes, meat, even fido meat. Yes, plenty of wide boys here, that is barrow boys, who know all the dodges.

On a good day at the market you may even see a perlie (a cockney wearing pearl buttons), a sort of cockney royalty. Perlies date back to the 19th century, when an enterprising cockney began collecting old buttons. Today, the title of perlie is almost hereditary, and perlies play an active role in East End charities.

At last I found a stand selling flowers. The proprietor wore a fine wool cap. He had a ruddy face, large blue eyes, and the strong nose that some say dates from the Roman settlement of Londinium. His wife seemed a shorter, bosomed, aproned twin.

"Six roses, please," I said. "Yellow."

"Ow many?"

"Just six."

"Oh, it's alf a country cousin you want. Ow much, bugs?" he asked his wife.

"Make it a pair of Alan Whickers," she answered.
"My bottle."
"Ave a butchers at 'is whistle. 'E's no deaf."
"That's why I need me trouble. Pardon me, two quid, sir," said the man.
"Two quid, it is," I said, "and two more if you'll translate what you said."
"Why that's just backchat."
The man explained that cockney slang developed to fool the bobbies—and that cockneys use it still when they don't want to be understood. But this good soul was happy to translate. I paid him and went on.

I headed back to Hyde Park, then to the Serpentine, and at last on to the boathouse. For a moment I didn't see Jenny anywhere. All around, couples were taking advantage of the fine weather, putting the rowboats to good use. And then Jenny came marching up in a bright yellow outfit, the picture of health.

"Jenny, how have you been?"
She leaned forward, and I kissed her on the cheek. I presented her with the roses.
"Thank you. Oh, they match! I've been OK, John. I'm glad to see you. I'm taking a bit of a risk, but we'll be all right."
"You have to tell me what all this is about. Really, Jenny, you've more than piqued my curiosity."
She looked out at the Serpentine.
"I'd love to dive into that water," she said. "Would you care to swim? People do. Even skinny-dip. Discretely." She looked over.

La Dolce Vita *in Kensington Gardens.*

"After you," I said as I pushed her toward the water.
"Stop," she laughed. "No. But we shall go rowing. Do you like to row?"

"Sure."

We rented a boat and began to row about the pond. At first, she insisted on rowing, but then I took over.

"Jenny, do you want to tell me where you've been? Or who you are, or where you come from? I know absolutely nothing about you. Absolutely nothing, and I'm a reporter. I'm paid to find things out about people. I do it by instinct. And somehow my instincts aren't working. Why don't you begin by telling me where you're from?"

"You should have asked. I'm from Cairo."

"Cairo?"

"Yes."

"So that's why you have such an interest in antiquities. I do, too—as an amateur, of course. Where did you grow up? You speak perfect English."

"I grew up in England, John. You see, my father was English, and my mother was Egyptian. My mother died in childbirth, and my father was good enough to send me to school here. He was well on in years, and I saw little of him really. His great love was his work; he was quite famous really. A famous Egyptologist. He spent most of his time on digs. He'd send the Rolls around with a check, that sort of thing. I suppose I can't complain—although I've always felt he regarded me as more an inconvenience than anything else. Not so much of one on balance, though."

"What was his name?"

"Sir Aleicester Ball."

"Well, at least you got a good education. But what's all this about? Who's trying to harm you, Jenny?"

"That I can't tell you, John."

"What do you mean you can't tell me!" I threw down the paddles. "You tell me you're in danger, and then you say you can't tell me who's after you. And meanwhile I'm falling in love with you, goddamn it!"

The moment the words came out, I regretted them. But she seemed to take it well.

125

"John."

"What?"

"Don't worry about me. It won't do a bit of good to tell you. It won't help me; it might hurt me. And it might hurt you."

"Now you're worrying about me? I haven't opened that stupid bag, by the way. What's in it?"

"Don't open it! Nothing but some things that belonged to my mother. John, if I find out you've opened that bag, I don't think I shall be able to trust you. I've given you that because you're one of the few people I think I can trust. Though I've hardly met you. Let's go back."

I began rowing back to the shore.

After we'd returned the boat, she seemed to relax.

"Let's forget about all that and just be glad it's a sunny day."

She put her arm around me, and I put mine around hers. I was glad to forget about anything, anything but this warm, wonderful woman beside me. Around us, all was green, and I watched as the sun cast shadows about the bushes and trees. It was too good to be true. I could smell her hair, her perfume. She felt warm all along where we touched. We walked vaguely toward Marble Arch, where she said she would catch a taxi.

"I forgot—Speakers' Corner," I said as we approached.

"Let's listen, John," she said. We joined the crowd, wailing,

The northeast corner of Hyde Park (once the entrance to Buckingham Palace).

126

beseeching, heckling around 100 nodes of thought.

Speakers' Corner is a fascinating place. Here, every Sunday, people say what's on their minds. Of course, speech is not totally free. Policemen patrol, and it is forbidden to speak against the queen, to speak in favor of the IRA, or to say anything blatantly against the police. Once I saw the police arrest a black speaker who had called them racist and urged supporters to riot. They hauled him off to a police van. Still, the institution seems marvelously developed, and most of the speakers are quite articulate.

As Jenny and I watched, we saw Moslems, American fundamentalists, Israelis, Christians, and a few people talking ordinary politics. Off to one side, a lord was speaking—Lord Sopor, a socialist and a Methodist minister. Several hecklers accused him of pederasty in the Parliament toilet.

Jenny and I paused before a Moslem dressed in a turban, holding a Koran, and being challenged by a red-cheeked, betweeded Englishman. The Moslem was arguing that everything in London was stolen. The Englishman replied, "Why did you let us steal it?"

"When the white man came to Africa, we had the land, and he had religion. When he left, we had religion, and he had the land. Let me tell you, if I were to meet my oppressor, I would not turn the other cheek."

The Englishman laughed and walked off. This struck a sour note to my ear. I looked at Jenny, but she was not paying attention. Something else was on her mind. She grabbed my lapel and turned us around.

"Let's go," she said, directing us toward the street.

"What?"

"No, don't turn around." We walked up to the street, where she hailed a cab, and I looked vainly around to try to see what she was running from.

I held her as she stood by the door of the cab.

"Jenny, tell me what's the matter!"

"Goodbye, John," she murmured, pulling free. I noticed that the flowers had fallen to the ground.

"Goodbye," she repeated.

"Claridge's," I shouted as an afterthought. She seemed to nod.

I let the door slam, and the car moved into traffic.

I turned to scan the crowd. And I saw someone familiar. It was just for a second, but I was sure I recognized him. I ran toward him, but it was no good. He was lost in the mob. But I was sure it was him. The skinhead from Victoria Gardens.

I felt distinctly uncomfortable. Why was London filled with these people? Perhaps I should have stayed in New York.

Strange ideas raced through my head. Just who was this woman? Why did she fascinate me? I tried to abandon the questions—to turn away from them as I might draw back from a bar in a bad neighborhood. Yet, my reporter's instincts told me that something was not right. I pictured Nigel, playing Hamlet, wrinkling up his nose and exclaiming, "Something is rotten in the city of London."

What a worn-out quote. Nigel would have come up with something better. "That one may smile, and smile, and be a villain. At least I am sure that it may be so...."

Where was that from, I wondered? The prince of Denmark again?

I thought a moment about the Bard of Avon, shuffling down these streets before shuffling off this mortal coil. Every line he wrote now recited, again and again, by Nigel and countless others.

But oh what lines!

"Oh that this too too solid flesh would melt"..."To be or not to be"..."Speak the speech, I pray you." Where was Nigel, now that I needed him?

All of these Shakespearean lines are as smooth and worn as the cobblestones of Covent Garden. But they are mouthed now like the liturgy of a church service, King James version, by people in awe of the sound but often ignorant of the sense.

And here I am, as ignorant as any. "How weary, stale, flat, and unprofitable/Seem to me all the uses of this world."

I felt like a character in a worn-out cliché of a story. Not Lear, not Hamlet. More like the protagonist from an Agatha Christie or Dashiell Hammett novel. Middle-aged man meets young, beautiful, exciting woman. Middle-aged man falls for woman. Middle-aged man doesn't know exactly what he's getting into.

Wait a minute, I thought to myself, remembering Humphrey

Bogart's character in *The Maltese Falcon*. Forget Shakespeare. I came here to write a simple guidebook. I had a good job and a good life, and then this dame entered the picture. And suddenly I don't know which way is up.

What would Humphrey Bogart do in a situation like this? I decided it was time to find a pub and have a stiff drink.

* * *

London's pubs

In my opinion, the public house, or pub, is London's greatest institution. Some may argue that Parliament was a greater innovation—or Oxford or the gentleman's club—but (and maybe it's the American in me) my vote goes to the pub. It's London's most democratic institution. "No greater institution has ever been developed to further human happiness than that of a good public house," the wise Dr. Johnson wrote. And when it's raining outside, or chilly, or just dark, a pub provides a feeling of warmth, welcome, and hospitality you can find nowhere else.

Until recently, many pubs had different sections: a public bar for tradesmen and a saloon, or lounge bar, for gentlemen. The saloon was often for men only (until feminists challenged this tradition in the 1970s). A trace of the class system remains in many pubs, where you may see signs reading, "The management regrets that those wearing soiled clothes or shoes shall not be served." (However, these signs frequently disappear on Thursday and Friday, when workmen traditionally are paid.)

Those located near tube stops tend to be the most public of pubs, because people stop in for a pint (or two) on the way to or from their train. Because these pubs change clientele hourly, they are good places to meet Londoners. The atmosphere is cosmopolitan and open.

Pubs more out of the way are frequented by nearby residents. Everyone in London has a local pub, chosen for its proximity to home—Londoners like convenience. At the local pub, you can find the local postman as well as resident journalists and businessmen. Everyone is welcome.

A word on real ales, which have recently made a comeback. The large breweries, such as Guiness, Bass, and Carlsberg, sell American-style beer pressurized in kegs. In this beer, the yeast has been killed through filtration or pasteurization, and the beer has become inert. Real ale is actually alive, the brew continuing to ferment. As a result, the publican must take special care of real ale—it must be sold neither too early nor too late. At its best, the flavor is marvelous. (You can recognize real ale by the large hand pump sticking up in the air—keg beers have simple taps.)

Once upon a time (before World War I), London's pubs were open 19 1/2 hours a day. Pub hours were cut to 5 1/2 during the war, and—like the empire—have never recovered. Recently, pubs were reopened during the afternoon, but they still close at 11 p.m. (which allows you to catch the tube and the English to make it to work the next morning). A bell sounds 10 minutes before closing time, signaling last call. The English, however, do not believe in ordering a last one and sipping it. At 11, publicans begin driving out their clients like collies driving the sheep. Lights flash, as barkeeps hoist chairs onto the tops of tables. The law affords you 10 minutes "drinking-up time," so don't be intimidated by the bell. But after the drinking-up time has passed, you are in violation of the law—and in trouble with your publican.

Between pints you may be invited to take part in a game of darts, an important part of the pub tradition. The British dart board is the same as that found in America. Each player gets three darts per turn, and the idea is to work your way from 201 points down to 0. To start the countdown, you must hit a double (the outer rim); you often must finish with a double as well. The middle rim counts triple; the bull's eye counts 25 (outer) or 50 (inner). Other popular pub games include shove-ha'penny, cribbage, ring the bull, and bat-and-trap—ask someone to explain the rules before you try to play.

In addition to beer, ale, and stout, pubs also serve gin and whiskey (from Scotland and Ireland), sold in measures of one-eighth of a gill (about one ounce). Try a single-male scotch, such as Glenfidditch or Loch Moran. Among Irish whiskies, Jameson's is popular, but less well-known brands also can be good. And don't miss an opportunity to try some of the West Country's excellent ciders. A popular brand is Strongbow.

Good pubs in London include:

- **Audley,** *South Audley Street, Mayfair.*

During one of England's periodic Puritan purges, the Victorians closed all the pubs in Mayfair. The duke of Westminister permitted the Audley to reopen, providing the pub was redecorated. However, he rejected the architect's original plans, which he thought made the pub "look too much like a gin palace." Finally, the duke agreed to a plan of renovation, and the Audley remains an outstanding example of classic Victorian design. The tasteful, high-ceilinged Audley is a pleasant place to have a drink. At lunchtime, carved sandwiches served in the pub surpass the uneven restaurant fare upstairs.

- **Cheshire Cheese,** *5 Little Essex St.; tel. 836-2347.*

A dark, old bar up an alley off Fleet Street, the Cheshire Cheese was patronized by Dr. Johnson, Samuel Pepys, W.B. Yeats, and, until recently, journalists. The many tourists somehow have not affected the pub's character, which is dark, rich, and inviting.

- **El Vino's,** *47 Fleet St.; tel. 353-6786.*

Situated on the river side of Fleet Street, this was once the journalists' hangout par excellence—and those scribes who remain in the area still patronize El Vino's. Women may not be served at the bar (they must drink sitting down)—a tradition that is in apparent violation of the law. This pub is filled with history and character.

- **Lamb and Flag,** *33 Rose St.; tel. 836-4108.*

This quaint little pub is situated up an alley where a gang of thugs hired by a countess once tried to beat Dryden to death after he wrote unflatteringly about the woman. (They only managed to put him in the hospital.) The back room, once frequented by Middle Temple lawyers and today filled with media types, with its open fire, was described by Dickens in *Bleak Street.* Small and crowded, the Lamb and Flag is definitely worth a stop. A good place for a friendly game of darts.

- **Marquess of Anglesea,** *39 Bow St.; tel. 240-3216.*

A block from Covent Garden, this pub is a cut above most others in the area. Journalists, actors, and businessmen getting off work vie for space at the bar or settle down at the comfortable tables in the back.

- **Museum Tavern,** *49 Great Russell St.; tel. 242-8987.*

Opposite the British Museum, this fine old pub combines warmth, hospitality, and beauty. Tourists do not overwhelm scholars from across the street, local residents, and an unusually literate collection of Londoners. Karl Marx is supposed to have had an occasional pint here—it certainly would have been convenient—and Cassanova pursued his exploits at the Museum Tavern (in its previous incarnation). Decent pub food at reasonable prices is available for lunch and dinner.

• **Nag's Head,** *10 James's St.; tel. 836-4678.*

This brightly lit pub is filled to the brim with young people—carrying on as they will. It is particularly crowded on weekends.

London's wine bars

If you tire of the raucous atmosphere of the city's pubs, look instead for a wine bar, where the atmosphere is generally relaxed and can be quite romantic. Women trying to escape the attentions of men also may prefer the wine bar to the pub.

London's popular wine bars include:

• **Brahms and Liszt,** *19 Russell St.; tel. 240-3661.*

The name of this rowdy wine bar has an interesting history. *Liszt* is Cockney rhyming slang for *pissed,* meaning drunk.

• **Coconut Grove,** *Barrett Street.*

• **Dorchester,** *Park Lane.*

• **Ebury Wine Bar,** *139 Ebury St., Belgravia; tel. 730-5447.*

This is one of the city's trendiest wine bars.

• **Peppermint Park,** *Upper St. Martin's Lane.*

• **Pheasantry,** *152 Kings Road.*

Mixed drinks are served in large cups sized like brassieres.

Chapter VIII

London is not the place to go in search of a café for breakfast. No, better to eat a full breakfast in your hotel, enjoy your tea or coffee there, and then go out for a morning constitutional. Visit the parks and the shops and revel in the history of the city. And when you tire, stop to enjoy a pint.

I was returning to my hotel after just such a pleasant walk through Mayfair, topped off with a bitter at the South Audley Pub, when the concierge handed me a message. It was what I'd been waiting for. "Meet me at Harrods, the Terrace restaurant, at 3. Jenny."

I washed up in my room, then made my way to the National Portrait Gallery, where I thought I might while away a couple of hours. I found a series of portraits of the Ball family, one of whom was chancellor of the exchequer around the turn of the century, a few others of whom served in the military.

At about 2:30 I took a cab over to Knightsbridge. I got out in front of the giant department store—a full block long, the largest in the world—and hustled through the throngs past the first of the food halls to the elevators, which I took to the fourth floor. After a short hike, I arrived at the restaurant, a small bar and glass-enclosed terrace decorated in brass, marble, wicker chairs, and plants. Jenny was out by the glass sipping tea at a table draped in linen. I sat down.

"You look all in a huff," she said over her teacup.

"Oh. Pardon me." I ran a hand through my sweaty hair. "I just got your message."

"Were you worried about me?"

"Yes, quite frankly."

"You needn't be. I'll make out. I always have."

"Does that mean..." I stared her right in the eye. But at that moment the waiter appeared. I ordered the full cream tea.

"Does that mean you're considering telling me what all this is about?" I continued.

"If you have a question, don't be shy. Ask. Go ahead. Ask me anything."

"Well to start with, where have you..."

"Mr. Woods, did anyone ever tell you you're a very handsome man?"

"Oh, stop it." For some reason, I was in no mood for her new mood—cute. "Where have you been?"

"Well, John, I had to go away. It had to do with my...family."

"Your father?"

"Yes." She looked around. At the tables near us were seated well-appointed pairs of women and the occasional tourist couple. Behind us, the pale red Victorian cornices beneath a salt and pepper sky reminded me of Mary Poppins. It was not a bad place to have a conversation. And some of our neighbors, all within eavesdropping distance, looked like they were interested in more than tea.

"Or not really my father. My brother. That is, my...half-brother. You see my father had, well when he had, that is when he and my mother...met, he was already married, back in England. My mother worked on his dig. But he had a family back in London."

"But what does that have to do with the trouble you're in? Is your father here?"

"My father is dead." She looked up quickly. The waiter had appeared, holding a silver tray. On the tray was a silver teapot and a china cup and saucer. He put those down, along with a plate of tiny sandwiches, one of salmon, the others of cucumber, egg salad, and cheese. When the waiter withdrew, Jenny continued.

"He died. And my brother inherited his estate. Well, a month ago, my...brother's butler uncovered, that is, he found some treasures in a safe in the study. They had belonged to my father, and, anyway, I had reason to believe there were people who wanted me to...Try the sandwiches."

Across from us a dowager burdened with shopping bags had adjusted her hat to hear us.

"Maybe we should talk about this elsewhere," Jenny whispered.

"Yes. By the way, I saw some of your family today. At the National Portrait Gallery."

"Finish your sandwiches."

"Fine." I devoured them. The waiter responded by bringing a tray of pastries, to which he suggested I help myself. I did.

"So your father's son—by his first marriage—is somehow involved," I said, biting into a cream puff.

"John."

"What?"

She reached up with her napkin and wiped the side of my mouth.

"Stop it, and tell me what happened."

"Well, it's not so much him as these people I know."

"Who? One of them is a skinhead."

"How did you know?"

"I saw him...first at Westminster and then the other day. But Jenny...have they threatened you?" I blurted.

"No. Or yes. John, I don't want to talk about it. But I thought I might take you by my stepbrother's place. He and his wife are at home today from 2 to 6. It's nearby. All right?"

"I'll take that as a no. And all right."

We settled our bill and descended some escalators. On the way down, Jenny asked me if I would ask her stepbrother something for her—whether we could see the antiquities or whether they were out in the country. She said she'd ask him herself, but it was a sore point. Outside, we took a cab a short distance to nearby Belgravia. Flowers on people's window sills provided the only breaks of color from the endless white of the houses and the sky above.

In front of one of these identical slices of the wedding cake, the cab stopped, and we got out. We rang the doorbell, and a gracious butler admitted us to the foyer. We made our way into the drawing room, where a variety of well-turned-out people stood in groups. It was everything an English drawing room should be, decorated in lemons, oranges, and beige. The looks we received were decidedly ambiguous. But Jenny was not to be put out. Grabbing my arm, she marched me up to a tall, rather dull-looking man with thinning hair dressed in a gray flannel suit.

"Prescott, I want you to meet a dear friend of mine from America, Mr. John Woods."

"Delighted to meet you, Mr. Woods."

"John is working on a book about London. We were just in the neighborhood, and, well, John is an expert on Egyptian antiquities. I insisted he come by."

"Is that so?" From Prescott's response, she might have said I had come to steal his silver.

"Tell Mr. Woods about the marvelous treasure you found recently."

"Oh. Well." With the air of someone telling an insurance agent what was lost, Prescott Ball proceeded to tell me how a butler tidying up his study out in the country had found an old safe containing treasures his father the Egyptologist had brought back from Egypt. "We're putting the pieces up for sale at Christie's next Wednesday," he said conclusively.

"Are they here? May I see them by any chance? Or is the treasure out in the country?"

He looked at me rather curiously. 'Some pieces are at Christie's. The more valuable ones are in the country. Under guard," he added. At that moment, the door chimed, and Prescott looked up over my shoulder. "Excuse me. Very nice to have met you, Mr...."

"Woods."

"Olivia," I heard him call as he walked over to greet a flamboyant, behatted woman in a cape.

"Prescott, dear, dear Prescott, it's so good to see you," this woman called, lavishing attention on the dull lord. It struck me that this woman was managing to animate him to something near a normal state. And then I saw something. His eyes smiled like Jenny's.

"Did you ask him?" whispered Jenny, taking my arm.

"Yes, I did."

"Very well, let's go."

"So soon?"

"You wish to stay?" she whispered.

"No."

"Lady Hollingsworth," exclaimed Jenny to the woman in the hat.

"Hello," said her ladyship. Jenny shook her rather limp, extended hand.

"A friend from America, John Woods—who is here to pursue an interest in Egyptian antiquities."

"Really," said Lady Hollingsworth, redirecting her hand. I discovered it was cool as well as bony.

"Well, not exactly. I'm writing a book."

"How marvelous." She threw back her cape. "On Egypt?"

"No."

"That's perfectly wonderful."

"Lady Hollingsworth, Prescott, I'm afraid my friend and I must be off," Jenny interjected.

"Oh, I'm so sorry. So nice to have met you, Mr...."

"Woods. John Woods."

"And, well, good luck on your book. Egypt is so fascinating. It was a great fascination of Sir Aleicester, you know."

"Indeed..."

"Erhh, yes. Nice to have," said Prescott. Lady Hollingsworth nodded as Jenny's half-brother steered her into the drawing room and Jenny and I walked out.

Outside, I was glad to breathe the cool, damp air. "That was...interesting," I said.

"Yes, aren't they awful? But what did he say?"

I looked at her. "Why do you care?"

Cleopatra's Needle, an authentic Egyptian obelisk, is flanked by two 19th-century British-made sphinxes.

"Don't be daft."

"In the country."

She smiled. "That's where I'd like to go this afternoon. Except for the weather." She looked up at the white sky. "Or do you have something else planned?"

"No, not really." But then something clicked. "Well, I have an idea."

"You do?"

"Yes. Shall we go to the next best thing, a park?"

"Why not?"

We made our way over to St. James's Park and for an hour or so walked around amongst all the green. Some ducks were doing the same. "What did one duck say to the other when it rained?" I asked.

"Nice day for a picnic," said Jenny laughing.

"Nobody but the rosebush knows how good mud feels between the toes," I rejoined. It struck me how she from Egypt and I from New York shared the same memories of English rhymes.

It didn't rain, but in the wet light the flowers seemed more vivid and the colors more marvelous. I saw a duck wander off the path and ran over to catch it. Unfortunately, I slipped and fell and got mud all over my jacket.

Jenny laughed. We sat down on a bench to clean off my jacket. We brushed off the dirt and laughed. And I kissed her.

We had dinner back at my hotel. As she left, she told me to call her soon. When she was gone, I sat alone for a while and marveled at this all. It was quite gone from my mind that she was in danger. All my doubts were allayed. Well, almost.

But as I continued to sit there, something beckoned. Finally, I gave in and went to the closet to get Jenny's bag. I got it out and opened it. I found only clothing at the top and put the bag back. I guess I wanted to suspend my critical faculties. Later that day I took the bag over to Jim MacAllister's place and decided to forget about it.

The next day I called Jenny's number. The recording said the number had been disconnected. She had slipped away again. I guess I wasn't meant to find romance and mystery in London, after all. Best to get back to the old guidebook. Let's see, where was I? Oh yes, entertainment—music, nightclubs, Soho, and sports.

* * *

Entertainment

Music

London has won fame in recent years for its rock groups, from the Beatles to the Rolling Stones to the Police. But long before people began worshiping the electric guitar, music filled London's halls and before that its churches.

Jazz

The **Camden Jazz Festival,** *the Roundhouse; tel. 267-2564; tube: Chalk Farm,* is held every year during July and August. But London is filled with good jazz year-round. Check out the following hot spots.

• **100 Club,** *100 Oxford St.; tel. 636-0933; tube: Oxford Circus.*

The 100 Club serves up good music and tasty food. Run by the Jazz Centre Society, it is less expensive than Ronnie Scott's. Jazz is presented every night except Tuesday and Thursday, which are reserved for rock.

• **Pizza on the Park,** *11 Knightsbridge; tel. 235-5550,* and **Pizza Express,** *10 Dean St., Soho; tel. 439-8722.*

An eccentric pizza maker has brought jazz to his pizza places. Pizza Express in Soho is a convenient place to stop after an evening at the theater (or after the pubs have closed). Admission is £5, the pizza is remarkably good, and the food and drinks are reasonably priced.

• **Ronnie Scott's,** *47 Frith St., Soho; tel. 439-0747; tube: Tottenham Court Road.*

This is the finest jazz joint in town, featuring American and British acts. Over the years it has played host to all the giants. An evening's bill usually includes both a singer and an instrumentalist. Drinks and food are reasonably priced, and there is no minimum. Check out the Downstairs Bar, a pine-paneled musicians' hang-out (you may recognize some of the faces here).

Nightclubs

London's nightclubs come in and out of fashion quickly—too quickly for my tastes. So when someone wants me to frequent a nightclub with him, I insist we stick to one of the following.

• **Annabel's,** *44 Berkeley Square, Mayfair; tel. 629-2350.*

This is the one club where you can disport yourself in the company of gentlemen—or even MPs. But when they leave, their children take over the place, along with wealthy developers and bookies. Memberships are difficult to come by, but ask a well-connected friend to invite you—I don't advise just showing up.

• **Camden Palace,** *1a Camden Road; tel. 387-0428; tube: Mornington Crescent* or *Camden Town.*

This disco was once a theater.

• **Comedy Store,** *28a Leicester Square; tel. 839-6665.*

This club offers good comedy, a strange audience, a bar, and food. Consult *Time Out* or *City Limits* for information on who's performing.

• **Hippodrome,** *Charing Cross Road and Leicester Square; tel. 437-4311.*

The Hippodrome is dependably noisy. Large, swirling lights descend from the ceiling, fog machines fill the place with smoke, and go-go dancers enliven the rafters. The clientele, which is young and well-dressed, changes nightly (Monday is gay night, for example). However, weekends draw a general crowd. Drinks are reasonably priced, and food is served at tables overlooking the dance floor.

• **Marquee,** *90 Wardour St.; tel. 437-6603.*

This rock club, a legend from the 1960s, is popular among young people.

• **Rock Garden,** *6-7 Piazza, Covent Garden; tel. 240-3691.*

New wave bands, including the Police, have got their starts here. (Upstairs, this Covent Garden café serves credible hamburgers and offers a view of the piazza.)

• **Stringfellow's,** *16-19 Upper St. Martin's Lane; tel. 240-5534.*

Peter Stringfellow owns both Stringfellow's and the Hippodrome. At Stringfellow's, the effect is high-tech chrome and velvet, and the crowd is a notch more sophisticated than at the Hippodrome. Dress appropriately—preferably in black.

• **Wag,** *35-37 Wardour St.; tel. 437-5534.*
The Wag is a punk club.
For more up-to-the-minute information on London's nightclubs, consult *The Face* or *Blitz*. These magazines explain the differences between acid house and house, between pogo and punk. (People of my generation may be more interested in *Harper's* or *Queen*.) Or read Nigel Dempster's column (the venerable Dempster coined the term Sloane Ranger and other media buzz words). London nightclubs change names not only in accordance with British fads, but also to avoid taxes and creditors.

Soho

"No sex, please, we're British," goes the phrase. However, for years, Soho, settled by Huguenots fleeing France after the Revocation of the Edict of Nantes in 1685, seemed to defy that rule. No longer. Under the current government, the postwar spirit of tolerance has given way to one that more closely resembles Victorianism. Soho's prostitutes are virtually gone. The remaining streetwalkers are in the business of collecting money and disappearing, which, paradoxically, is a lesser offense than prostitution.

In the same spirit, the area's sex shops stock fewer and less explicit materials, and business has generally declined. The result is that reputable businessmen have abandoned the business completely to outright criminals.

Because nudity is illegal, £1 bed or peep shows consist of a dressed girl sitting on a bed. The idea is to lure you inside, where you are served expensive cocktails. If a hostess sits down with you, you are also billed for her company and her drinks. In a matter of minutes, the bill can climb to hundreds of pounds— and a group of thugs will arrive to collect it. Why does the government permit these clip joints to stay open, while it closes more innocent businesses? It seems to

The parish of St. Anne, Soho.

hope that by making sex criminal, people will begin to avoid it.

One establishment has retained a decent reputation. **Raymond's Revue Bar,** *6 Walker's Court; tel. 734-1593,* offers a plush if downscale imitation of the Paris Lido or Crazy Horse.

Soho's sex clubs advertise in *Time Out, City Limits,* and particularly *What's On.* If you ask a cab driver which clubs you should visit, he will take you where he gets the biggest commissions (he may do this even if you give him the address of where you want to go).

Sports

Cricket

Two types of cricket are played in London: one-day cricket and three-day test matches. Test matches between top commonwealth teams sell out way in advance. Tickets are £4 to £7.

Lord's, *St. John's Wood Road; tel. 289-16151; tube: St. John's Wood,* is the place to see cricket. Home of the Marylebone Cricket Club (MCC), Lord's is a hallowed place to some. South of the river, the Surrey Cricket Club sponsors test matches at the **Oval,** *Kennington; tel. 582-6660.*

Cricket is similar to baseball. (Die-hard cricket fans will tell you their sport is more difficult to play than baseball—to which I reply that it is only more difficult to watch. I'm kidding, though. The game makes civilized outdoor viewing, and the general atmosphere is relaxing.) Basically a bowler bowls a ball to a batsman standing by a wicket. Wickets are stick-like bases (cricket has two, not four, as in baseball). Usually, the batsman tries to hit the ball. However, sometimes, particularly in test matches, a team will play for a draw, a very English if slow-paced experience. The idea is for the batsman (not to mention the fans) to stay up (at bat) indefinitely. Runs often number in the hundreds.

The **Cricket Memorial Gallery** (adjacent to Lord's), which is open match days from 10:30 a.m. to 5 p.m., houses cricket memorabilia, including the ashes of a wicket stump played for in test matches.

Gather pre-game victuals at the Chapel Street Market, near St. John's Wood.

Equestrian events

Mid-June is Ascot, while early June is Derby (pronounced Darby). In late July, the Royal International Horse Show showcases the best of the world's show jumping.

Football

Although British football (American soccer) is a comparatively peaceful sport, English fans supply the violence themselves. Despite efforts to end hooliganism, it remains epidemic. Gangs of fans in colored scarves cheer their teams aggressively from the sidelines. The biggest matches take place at Wembley Stadium. For local contests, buy your ticket at the gate (£3 or £4) an hour beforehand, but for international matches, consult a ticket agent. For more information, contact the **London Football Association,** *tel. 690-9626.*

Rowing

The Henley Regatta is the granddaddy of London's rowing events. In late June or early July, the best teams in the world take to the Thames in an unparalleled display of oarsmanship. Even my publisher's hometown, Baltimore, Maryland, sends a team to compete. Tickets (£3) are usually available. For information, call *04912-21-53.* To get to the event, take British Rail from Paddington to Henley.

Rowing on the Thames.

Rugby

Rugby is the English equivalent of American football. Played in the

143

cold, wet months of September through April, it has enough violence to satisfy the most enthusiastic sports fan. The idea is to throw, carry, or kick a ball across a goal line. Amateur matches take place at Twickenham. The professional version (which is slightly different) is played at Wembley. For more information, contact the **Rugby Football Union,** *Whittan Road, Twickenham; tel. 892-8161.*

Swimming

The British swim slowly, in swan-like, regal motions. But they don't seem to mind if you pass them. Following are some places to swim.

• **Berkeley Hotel,** *Wilton Place; tel. 235-6000.*

The Berkeley Hotel offers (somewhat expensive) public swimming in its pleasant pool in Knightsbridge.

• **Champneys Health Club,** *Meridien Piccadilly Hotel, 21-22 Piccadilly; tel. 439-0008 or 494-1256.*

This is probably the best swimming and health club in Britain—although you must stay at Champneys (or join the club; a one-year membership costs £900) to take advantage of it. The clear, inviting pool is bedecked with classical statues and uses the new hypocell purification system, which is superior to chlorine.

When you tire of swimming, take advantage of the extensive weight room, saunas, Turkish baths, dance studio, and army of experts and masseuses. The club also has squash courts, snooker tables, a restaurant, writing desks, and even a library stocked with newspapers.

Ironically, the British have declined to take advantage of the Champneys Health Club—the atmosphere is a bit too lush—but local Americans and Japanese keep it busy.

• **Crystal Palace National Sports Centre,** *Ledrington Road; tel. 778-0131.*

The Crystal Palace National Sports Centre has a clean, Olympic-sized pool (£1.25), squash courts (£2 per half-hour, plus 40p a day for membership), and generally excellent facilities.

• **Fitness Centre,** *11-13 Floral St.; tel. 836-6544.*

I'm told women love the Fitness Centre. Situated on a street formerly renowned for dance, due to its proximity to the Royal Opera House, the center provides full beauty treatments, as well as dance and athletic facilities. In addition, both men and women can swim in the pool and use the gymnasium next door. Membership is £12 a day, and access to the swimming pool is £5. The Fitness Centre is open Monday through Friday from 7 a.m. to 9 p.m.; Saturday and Sunday from 10 a.m. to 6 p.m.

• **Highgate Pond,** *tel. 340-4044; tube: Highgate* (men only), and **Kenwood Ladies' Pond,** *tel 340-1033; tube: Hampstead Heath* (women only).

• **Oasis,** *32 Endell St.; tel. 836-9555.*

The Oasis is less expensive than Champneys. It has two good pools (one indoor, one outdoor), as well as a weight room and other gym facilities. Swimming costs £1.50.

• **Porchester Baths,** *Porchester Road; tel. 229-3226.*

The Porchester Baths, situated at the top of Queensway in Baywater, harken back to a former sleepy glory. In addition to a large tiled pool with a wooden gallery for spectators, there are Turkish baths and relaxation rooms (with beds) for bathers. The baths are alternately reserved for men and women—except on Sunday, which is co-ed.

• **Serpentine Lido,** *Hyde Park; tel. 262-5484.*

Outdoor swimming is offered here year-round (but only members of the Serpentine Swimming Club can swim in winter). Swimming is free before 9 a.m.

• **YMCA,** *112 Great Russell St.; tel. 637-8131; tube: Tottenham Court Road.*

The YMCA offers not only swimming, but also rock climbing, badminton, basketball, gymnastics, martial arts, aerobics, table tennis, volleyball, and yoga. A weekly membership costs £18.

Tennis

Wimbledon is the place for tennis. In late June and early July, crowds head to the famous courts to watch world professionals compete. Buy tickets to the matches (which cost £8 to £13) well before opening day. Or, if you're more interested in the spectacle than the tennis, simply buy a pass to enter the grounds (£5; £3 after 5 p.m.).

Chapter IX

A few days later, glancing through the *Times*, I was reminded of the auction of Egyptian antiquities at **Christie's,** *98 King St.; tel. 839-9060; tube: Green Park.* Auction listings are published Tuesday in the *Times,* Monday in the *Daily Telegraph.* (Christie's also has a second location, in South Kensington, *85 Old Brompton Road.*)

The next morning, wearing my Sunday best, I took a cab down to St. James's. The auction room was predictably elegant. (The Christie's in South Kensington is less formal.) The auctioneer stood at a lectern at the front of the room. Television monitors were placed discreetly about to provide close-ups of the goods being auctioned.

The women in the room were dressed in pearled gowns and hats; the men wore morning suits. It did not seem odd at all that a Van Gogh sold here recently for $40 million. I made out Lord Prescott near the front and the hatted Lady Hollingsworth—but no sign of Jenny.

The auctioneer appeared. Staring over black reading glasses, he began by announcing that several lots had been withdrawn. No explanation. A slight gasp was heard throughout the room, but the auctioneer ignored it and immediately opened the bidding. He spoke in a series of grunts, addressing the crowd and then his list, moving the bids according to barely perceptible motions from the viewers.

It was a pity I hadn't seen Sir Aleicester's collection while it was on view, but even the pictures on the monitors told me it was priceless. But then Christie's specializes in pricing the priceless. On the block were the personal effects of kings and queens from the XVIII dynasty—amulets, earrings, bangles, beaded necklaces, and combs. The highlight was a model boat complete with a crew of slaves to row the pharaoh to the afterlife.

The auction proceeded rapidly, the goods fetching high prices

Retriever *by A.F. Desportes was sold at Christie's on June 19, 1988 for about FF2 million.*

from the well-heeled bidders. At last it was time to go. People rose from their seats, donning coats. I don't know what I had expected to find—Jenny perhaps—but I hadn't found it. Making my way over to Sir Prescott (who didn't seem particularly happy), I came face to face with Lady Hollingsworth.

"Lady Hollingsworth," I said.
"Isn't it terrible?" she asked.
"What?"
She narrowed her eyes. "The theft."

But I was distracted. Walking out ahead of us in a brown double-breasted suit was the sunglassed man I'd seen with Jenny. At least I thought it was him. An Arab, or maybe an Egyptian— the one driving the Jaguar.

The more I stared at the man, the more I was sure it was him. I apologized to Lady Hollingsworth and began forcing my way through the crowd. Outside, the man headed down the block, and I hurried after him. At the corner he turned, and I broke into a run. There it was, the green Jaguar. I came up as he was getting in on the right.

"Excuse me," I yelled, trying to catch my breath. He paused

and looked up. Was there a flash of recognition? It was impossible to tell with the sunglasses.

"Yes?" he said.

"You're a friend of Jenny Wilde."

"I'm sorry."

"Jenny Wilde. I need to find her."

"I know no such person. Excuse me." He began to close the door, but I reached out and grabbed it.

"You picked her up. I need to see her."

"Hey!" he yelled. I turned, but it was a trick. The door shut. As I rapped on the window, then banged, the Jaguar peeled out from the curb. I managed to catch its license plate number. Well, that was that. Once again, it seemed, I would have to wait.

In my charged-up condition, I decided to go for a walk—a long walk, down to the peaceful Mall (built in 1906 as a place for royal and state processions), then along St. James's Park in the direction of Buckingham Palace. Outside the palace were the usual hordes of tourists (they're always hanging about, even though the palace is closed to the public). The flag was flying, indicating that the queen was in town—back from her weekend in Windsor. I walked around the palace, along Buckingham Road, a rather dreary stretch past servants' quarters and stables.

I was apprehensive. I couldn't shake the feeling that someone was following me. Then I noticed a white Rover behind me. I cut down a one-way street and watched from behind a tree. Yes, the car stopped. A man got out hurriedly and came trotting down from the corner. I turned and headed away. Looking over my shoulder, I saw that the man had speeded up to follow. I broke into a run and turned at the first corner. I pulled up quick. Was it the Arab? There were bushes at the side of the building. I stepped behind them to hide and wait. When the man's foot appeared, I made my move, tackling him at the waist and wrestling him down to the concrete, grabbing an arm and then a hand. From my days playing (American) football, I remembered how to take a man to the ground. I used all my weight to pin him down and restrain his hands. No chance for him to reach for a gun.

"Who are you?" I yelled. "What do you want from me?"

"Stop! Stop it! You're in big trouble!" he complained, utterly surprised. It was almost with curiosity that I beheld a policeman moments later, looming over us in blue.

"Officer!" I yelled. The bobby stared down intensely. "Officer, this man was chasing me down the street."

"Get up, both of you," the bobby demanded, producing his billy club. "Up!"

"You are in big trouble, sir," said the man I'd wrestled to the ground. He was not the Arab at all. He wore a suit that didn't fit him particularly well. Beyond that, he was rather nondescript, heavyset, with brown medium-length hair and a flat nose. He began brushing the dust off his clothes.

"Shut up, you," said the bobby to him after observing our respective appearances.

"Shut up, me?" He looked at the bobby, then reached into his jacket. "MI5," he snarled, producing a badge.

The bobby's eyes shifted from him to me. He began to look rather violent.

"What's the meaning of this?" I yelled.

"I think you'll find out quick enough. Officer, take custody of this man." The bobby grabbed my arm.

"Grab the other one." The bobby complied.

The MI5 man stared right into my eyes and then, without warning, hauled off and hit me. The two took me down to New Scotland Yard on Victoria Street, where an Inspector Bosdale questioned me. When I explained that I was a reporter from New York staying at Claridge's, they seemed to reconsider—at least Bosdale seemed to reconsider.

Scotland Yard.

"You'll have to forgive us, Mr. Woods, the atmosphere right now being what it is."

The MI5 man, though, was less conciliatory. He explained that he'd seen me talking to the man in the Jaguar, who was suspected of being an art thief.

"Art thief?"

"Yes, specializing in Egyptian antiquities. You may remember that several lots were withdrawn from the auction at Christie's. The truth is, those goods were stolen yesterday from the Ball's estate in Kent. We believe that one of the thief's biggest customers may be the Egyptian government itself, but we don't have any proof."

"I see. I'm terribly sorry."

"But why did you run up to talk to him?"

"That's very simple." I was about to tell them about Jenny when...I didn't. "I thought I recognized him from Cairo. A long ways back. I was there during Sinai."

"Really, you were there in Sinai?"

"Yes."

"It's obvious Mr. Woods knows nothing about this," said Bosdale.

"That long ago? You thought you remembered him?"

"Well, yes."

"Sinai, a sad outcome that. Of course, we would hardly expect a man of your background to be involved in a jewel theft, would we?" chimed in Bosdale.

"A word of advice, Mr. Woods," said the MI5 man. "Stay out of trouble. I'm sorry about the black eye, but then you gave me quite a run for my money. American football, eh?"

"British boxing?" I asked. "Queensberry rules?"

"Well, not quite. But are we even?"

"I guess so."

"Oh, one other thing, Mr. Woods," added the MI5 man. "Now that they know who you are, don't be foolish."

"What do you mean?"

"They don't want trouble. So you can forget this ever happened. But if you do see them again, call Inspector Bosdale." He motioned, and Bosdale handed me a card. "I must remain undercover."

And with that they let me go.

Outside, the sun had come out. I felt exhausted but free. I walked vaguely in the direction of Victoria, but then I had an idea. Why not go to Kew Gardens? Maybe the plants would give me some consolation—the sheer natural beauty, you know. From Victoria, I jumped on the District Line tube (Richmond Branch) out to Kew. Thirty minutes later, I got off and circled under the tracks to the village. Groups of tourists streamed in both directions down the small, tree-lined street that runs from the village square to the gardens, passing in front of people's living rooms. But the residents, despite the seeming invasion of their privacy, couldn't be friendlier. I stopped in at **Hobson's,** *2 Station Parade,* to buy some victuals, then continued down to the gate.

Inside, I wandered awhile, looking at the palms, the swans, the giant tropical lilies, the plants with six-foot leaves in the heated Princess of Wales Conservatory. I lingered over the papyrus plants, which have always interested me. The foundation, after all, of paper. The trip was not quite working, though. The couples enacting the rites of spring on the park benches made me think, alas, of Jenny. All of them imitating the blooming of the flowers.

The bench I sat on was dedicated to a man "who in his life, loved this place." How British, I thought, not necessarily positively. I decided to lay down on the grass instead (the hell with my clothes and decorum), which was shaved as low as a golf green. I stared at the sky until it decided to cloud over. Only in England.

(Kew Gardens is open from about 9:30 a.m. to dusk—the closing hour changes seasonally. Admission is £1.)

On the way back to the gate, it began to rain, and I ducked into **Kew Greenhouse,** *1 Station Parade,* to wait it out. After the rain had let up a bit, I caught the tube. When I heard all the foreign accents up on the street, I knew I was back in London.

ROYAL BOTANIC GARDENS KEW

All I could think of was getting back to the hotel and asking room service for some ice. From the looks I was getting, it was clear my eye had swollen menacingly. A glass of whiskey would do for the pain. At Claridge's the doorman opened the door, discretely avoiding my eye. I picked up my key from the concierge.

"Would you like some ice, sir" the friendly woman asked. Or perhaps," she hesitated, "...even a doctor?"

"Yes, some ice would be nice. And a bottle of scotch." I crossed the black and white marble to the elevator. Upstairs, I took out my key, opened the door, and entered my suite. I walked through the foyer, opened the door to the living room, and flipped on the light.

In an armchair sat the man in sunglasses, holding a pistol aimed at my head. From behind me, in the bathroom, I heard a noise. I turned and stared in amazement. It was the skinhead. He smiled to reveal several missing front teeth.

"Welcome, Mr. Woods," said the man in the chair. "We've been waiting for you."

* * *

Forgive me for interrupting my story again. However, we're getting near the end, and I've still much to tell you about London. The city's history, for example...

A bit of London's history

According to Prince Charles, "the city of London took 300 years to rebuild after the Great Fire of 1666, but only 15 years to destroy with oppressive concrete steel and glass towers. Can you imagine the Venetians building tower blocks next to San Marco?"

The name *London* comes from the Celtic *llyn* (lake) and *din* or *dun* (hill fort), indicating that this fortified village rose above the Thames marshes even before the Romans arrived—making London one of Britain's oldest cities. Confirmation of the city's antiquity came during World War II, when Celtic remains were uncovered.

However, like most British towns, London's recorded history goes back to Roman times. The city was a fortress abandoned by Suetonius, then rebuilt as Augusta. In the fourth century, a wall was erected around the Roman city, most of which corresponded to what is still called London Wall in the City. One of the old Roman gates was uncovered in the City at Bishopsgate about 1900. A Roman covered bridge spanned the area today occupied by London Bridge.

The Anglo-Saxons made London a city in A.D. 610 by designating St. Paul's Church a cathedral. The city's position as a major center of power was underscored when the Danes were expelled (A.D. 886) and a royal palace built outside its walls at the suburb of Westminster (by Ethelred, son of Alfred). In the 12th century, an observer described the palace as "an incomparable structure furnished with a breastwork and bastions at a distance of two miles from the city." Fitzstephen went on to write, "Adjoining to the houses on all sides are the gardens of those citizens that dwell in the suburbs, which are well-furnished with trees, spacious, and beautiful." (London is still blessed with garden suburbs, where its citizens reside.)

William the Conqueror granted London a charter, still kept in the Guildhall, significant because it was written in Anglo-Saxon, not French. During the Middle Ages, apart from fire, plague, and the odd insurrection (including Wat Tyler's in 1381), life was peaceful, and London was prosperous. By the time of the first Elizabeth, the old city walls had been breached by the expanding city—and the Royal Exchange had been built, marking London's move toward becoming the commercial center of Europe. Elizabethan Bloomsbury was really full of blooms, and Covent Garden was a garden. The population was just more than 150,000 after the first disaster, the Plague.

The Great Fire of 1666.

In 1666, the even more disastrous Great Fire almost totally destroyed the city both inside the Roman walls and in the surrounding areas, where the people lived in wooden houses close together. The act of parliament outlining the rebuilding of the city wisely required that all buildings be made of stone or brick. However, the Solons rejected a proposal by the great architect Sir Christopher Wren, who wanted to design a new street plan for London. As a result, the city was rebuilt as a muddle of old streets and new thoroughfares.

Despite plague and fire, by the late 17th century, the population of London had grown to more than a half-million, making it the largest city in Europe.

In the 18th century in London, as elsewhere, the aristocracy migrated westward—here settling Hyde Park and St. James's, still centers of smartness but no longer areas where people live. By the time of the first census in 1801 (which included St. Pancras, Marylebone, Paddington, and the rural edge of London, called Chelsea), the population was 860,035. In the 19th century, London gobbled up and consolidated Regent's Park, Belgravia, Westbourne, and Tyburnia north of the park, as well as the Great Wen (the phrase is not Prince Charles') and began to gobble up areas south of the Thames from Greenwich to Lambeth.

One of the problems with London is deciding where its borders are—and therefore the size of its population. The metropolitan police district covers a 15-mile radius around Charing Cross, encompassing 690

St. James's, a center of smartness.

square miles. The London postal zone covers a 9- to 10-mile radius, which it separates into a complex and unmemorizable set of postal zip codes based on the old system, which divided the area into geographic zones. One reason for the confusion is that the Greater London Council, which was dominated by leftists led by Kenneth "Red Ken" Livingstone, was abolished by Mrs. Thatcher; in its place has been put a more decentralized scheme. If you include areas from which commuters travel, London encompasses most of southeastern England.

However, greater London is largely not what tourists come to Britain to see. But it is worthwhile considering the lifestyle all that suburbia represents.

The British empire may be dead, the country's economic force spent, and the symbols of its power the subject of television serials, but the heritage of civilized housing can never be lost. The Englishman's home is not only his castle under law, but it also bears some of the features of a castle. It always is enclosed, in contrast to the rolling, borderless suburbs of the United States; it almost always has a yard, in Britain called a garden; and it almost always has an upstairs (the ranch style never made it here). In fact, the poor British forced to live in housing projects (called council flats) are considered particularly wretched because they do not have a private bit of soil and an upstairs to call their own. The British are the best-housed people in Europe. And they are much more comfortable (homely, in their confusing language) than the inhabitants of another overpopulated, damp island with major economic pretensions—Japan.

Chapter X

Writing a book about London was the last thing on my mind.

I stood there, dumbfounded. The Arabic-looking man in sunglasses motioned to the skinhead, who proceeded to close the door behind me.

"Have a seat," he directed. He wore a well-cut double-breasted suit, the same one he'd been wearing at the auction.

"Don't you ever take off your sunglasses?" I asked.

"Rarely." He laughed, showing white teeth. "Certainly not for you, Mr. Woods." He produced a pack of Players' cigarettes. "Oh, pardon me. Have you two been introduced? Mr. Woods, this is Wendell. Wendell, this is Mr. Woods. Do you smoke, Mr. Woods?"

"No. I quit."

"How healthy of you. I hope you remain in good health. Americans are always thinking about their health, aren't they?" He lit a cigarette with a gold lighter, inhaled, and flicked the ashes on the Oriental carpet. "I suppose they have people to clean the rugs," he said.

"I suppose you can explain what you're doing here in my hotel suite." My mind was racing. I felt like I was playing a part in a movie...*The Man Who Know Too Much*...like I was caught in a story of someone else's making. My palms were sweating. But the man in the chair seemed unconcerned.

"Don't be so nervous." He waved the gun. "And have a seat. You appear tired," he said. "And your eye is rather swollen."

"I thought guns were illegal in England," I said, choosing the other wing chair.

"Frankly, I don't know."

"Where is Ms. Wilde?" I asked.

"Oh, Ms. Wilde. She's fine. You'll meet her soon. I'm thirsty. Don't you have anything to drink? Maybe we should call room service or send Wendell out."

"If you want," I said, suddenly hopeful.

"No. That would be self-indulgent. And it would run up your tab. And poor Wendell. The management might not let him in. And that would be bad for his self-image. No, let's just get down to business. Tell me, Mr. Woods, where have you put the bag?"

"I don't know what you're talking about. How did you get in here?" I asked.

"Oh, no. I believe you will allow me to do the talking. Wendell."

I turned. There stood Wendell. Medium height. Shaved head. He had a smile tattooed on his forehead and was dressed in long underwear, ill-fitting fatigue pants, suspenders, and work boots laced up most strangely. What was most noticeable about him, though, was that he was missing two of the middle fingers of his right hand.

He came up next to me, pressed his face up to mine, and barked.

It was enough to make me look away.

"Wendell. Down Wendell," said the Arab.

"What's your name?" I asked.

"Mr. Ali will do. Now, you will do as I tell you, or I may let Wendell have his way. Wendell can be difficult to control. Such an emotional animal."

"What do you want?"

"The bag."

"I know nothing about it. I haven't looked in the bag. Ms. Wilde gave it to me to hold, that's all I know."

"Where is the bag, Mr. Woods?"

"I just told you, I don't have it."

"No?" From the other side of the room, I heard Wendell growl. "No, Mr. Woods?" Wendell's growling grew louder.

"Can you give him a bone or something?" I asked.

"I'm afraid that's just what he wants. Down, Wendell," said the Arab. Wendell's growl became a low, guttural grunt that ended in a sort of whimper. "One of yours. You observe Wendell's hand," said Ali.

"Yes."

"Let that be your warning. He may lack several teeth, but his bite remains strong. Now, shall we return to business?"

"I'll make you a deal. You take me to Ms. Wilde, prove she's OK, and you can have the bag. I don't want it."

"Mr. Woods, you are beginning to make sense."

"On one condition. You tell me what this is about. I think I already know what's in the bag. Egyptian artifacts, probably extremely valuable ones. If I'm not mistaken, they came from the collection of Sir Aleicester Ball. The question is, why did you give them to me? Or why did Ms. Wilde?"

"The answer is simple enough. And I don't mind telling you. You see, when you called Jenny, Mr. Woods, the coincidence of your having the same initials seemed too good to be true. What's more, you are a respected reporter. We have a problem, those of us in the business of antiquities. We are not allowed to transport the goods of our trade out of England. Money is not the problem. What we don't steal we can buy—except for what you see in the British Museum. But England has plenty of other priceless collections. However, London is an island and transport...inconvenient.

"But here was a tailor-made situation. The idea was for Jenny to give you a bag to hold for her. As a reporter, we assumed you would open it, whereupon you would have the opportunity to look at some of her clothing. Embarrassed, you would be unlikely to look again or to question Jenny further. Then Ms. Wilde would ask you to carry the bag through customs for her."

"Why would I do that?"

"Ms. Wilde can be very persuasive. Why not? You had begun to care for her, had you not? At the last minute, we intended to switch bags, taking the one with the clothing from you and leaving you with the one containing the valuables. Once you had passed through the barrier into the international departures area, our agent would take the bag and deliver it to our client in Cyprus."

"But how did you know they wouldn't check me? It happens."

"A calculated risk. But given your stature, unlikely. If they did catch you, you'd be called upon to explain. You might have talked your way through. Who knows? If not, you would have taken the rap.

"However, we encountered a little snag. Ms. Wilde decided to double-cross us. You see, she had some silly, patriotic idea of returning the gems to Egypt. Of course, she'd make out well enough. She gave you the real bag for safekeeping from us, confident she could convince you not to open it. She hid the valuables in a false bottom beneath some of her belongings. But then she began to go soft. She got the idea that you would hold the bag, then she would get it out of the country without putting you at risk."

"Where is Jenny?"

"I suppose you would like to see her."

"You bastard. I'll ring your neck if you've hurt her."

"I assure you, Jenny is quite alive. Wendell."

I looked up. The skinhead began to howl. Saliva appeared through his teeth. He turned and went out into the hall. There were noises in the bedroom. A moment later, he kicked open the door. I jumped up. It was Jenny, gagged and bound.

"Jenny!"

She nodded, eyes bright and wide.

"You bastards!"

"Wendell, the gag." The skinhead pulled off the gag, and Jenny looked at me. "Oh, John, they've got you, too."

"Careful, Mr. Woods," said the Arab, standing. "One false move, and Jenny is no more. You see, she has no more use to us except as concerns you. Now, where is the satchel?"

The doorbell rang.

"Who's that?" asked the Arab.

"It's someone from room service with ice."

"Get rid of him. If you say one word, that's the end of Ms. Wilde. Remember, you did not report any of this to the police when you were questioned. You are implicated. Tell whomever it is to come back in an hour."

My brain reeled.

"I'm right behind you," the Arab warned as I began walking toward the door. I walked past Jenny, stopping to look at her for a second. Her eyes hinted hope. Then I felt a hand on my shoulder.

"Wait. On second thought, Jenny, you go to the door."

"Never!"

"Never? Then I'll go myself."
He went to the door and said, "Come back later, please."
"Some ice, sir?"
"No."
"Very good, sir."
The Arab came back into the room, closing the door to the foyer behind him. Then he broke into laughter. "What a good joke. I enjoy a joke, don't you? Now, friends, let us decamp to where you have hidden the bag. Wendell will leave with Ms. Wilde. If we do not show up in 10 minutes, Wendell, you know what to do."
"And I'm wanting to do it."
I was surprised to hear that the monster could speak.
"Now, Mr. Woods, the address."
I gave them Jim MacAllister's address, then watched as they walked out the door. A few minutes later, I left the hotel with Ali.

* * *

Once again, I must interrupt my story to return to my guidebook. It's time to shop London's street markets. My favorite are listed below.

London's street markets

• **Bermondsey (New Caldeonian) Market,** *Long Lane and Tower Bridge Road; tube: Tower Bridge.*

Every Friday, shoppers rise long before dawn and carry their torches (flashlights) south of the river to the Bermondsey Market below Tower Bridge. From the tube, hike down Bridge Street and turn right into Bermondsey Square.

Goods at the Bermondsey Market are better quality than those at other markets in the city—hence the passion of the participants. By noon, the market is over.

• **Camden Lock,** *Camden High Street and Chalk Farm Road; tube: Camden Town.*

The weekend, especially Sunday, is the time to visit Camden Town. Stroll through this area, which retains an (authentic) Bohemian flavor.

Camden Town's market keeps more reasonable hours than the others. You can show up at 4 p.m. and still find plenty of merchandise to choose from.

From the tube at Camden Town, make your way up Camden High Street to Camden Lock (at the Regent's Canal). **Compendium Books,** *234 Camden High St.; tel. 267-1525,* is London's only literary bookstore (it sponsors poetry readings). A good bet for a meal is one of the many Greek/Cypriot restaurants in the area (try Nontas). Many of the residents (and pubs) in Camden are Irish.

• **Camden Passage,** *Islington; tube: Angel.*

More up-scale than the other street markets I've mentioned (and farther from the city), Camden Passage is known for its quality antiques, which are featured every Wednesday morning and Saturday. For coins, shop on Tuesday; for books, go on Thursday or Friday.

From the tube at Angel, stroll up Islington High Street (the best goods are farthest north). When you're hungry, visit the Camden Head Pub.

• **Greenwich,** *High Road; tube: New Cross* or *New Cross Gate.*

This market specializes in antiques, many with a nautical twist. Visit on the weekend, particularly Sunday.

• **Petticoat Lane,** *Middlesex Street; tube: Liverpool Street* or *Aldgate East.*

Petticoat Lane reminds me of Orchard Street in New York, this part of the East End corresponding to New York's Lower East Side. Come Sunday morning, cockney mingles with Jewish (many Jews settled here following the war) and Bengali or Arabic accents. Along Cheshire Street and Brick Lane, the market gets going at 4 a.m. (these people are serious shoppers). Flashlights are necessary. By 9 a.m., the hubbub in this area settles down, as Petticoat Lane proper (Middlesex Street) fills with shoppers. Also check out Cutler Street. By 2 p.m., the market is over.

Petticoat Lane specializes in new goods (many of them seconds); the other streets offer a potpourri of new and used merchandise.

Have lunch at nearby Blooms, where the line is part of the fun.

• **Portobello Road.,** *tube: Ladbroke Grove* or *Nottinghill Gate.*

Every weekend, Portobello Road comes alive with stalls selling every sort of merchandise. Paloma Picasso recently reported that she buys all her clothes here. However, the market is best known for its antiques and silver. From the tube at Nottinghill Gate, walk up Pembridge Street and turn left onto Portobello Road. You'll come to the antiques first, then the clothing, and finally the food. Try the crepes at Obelix.

Chapter XI

I suppose I might have nodded to the doorman or made a run for the house detective. I could have tried to write a note under some pretext or begun shouting in the lobby. But whether it was concern for Jenny's safety or simple journalistic curiosity, I didn't do any of those things. We walked around the corner to Ali's car.
"You drive," he said. "No, wait. Can you drive on the left?"
"It would be a shame if I crashed this heap."
"Yes, for Ms. Wilde."
I got in and began to drive. From Brook Street, I cut down past Berkeley Square to Piccadilly. I took a right down to Hyde Park Corner and then headed along Brompton Road to Kensington. We passed the pretty Brompton Oratory (a Catholic church built in the Italian baroque style). The Jaguar gave a smooth, comfortable ride. Had it not been for the circumstances, I might have enjoyed the tour.

Next, we passed Harrods, then, turning up Cromwell, the dazzling complex of Victorian buildings erected after the Great Exhibition of 1851, Prince Albert's crowning legacy (Victoria completed much of the construction). Along Cromwell are the Victoria and Albert Museum and the Natural History Museum. Farther back are the Geological Museum, the Science Museum, the Imperial College of Science and Technology, the Royal College of Music, and the Royal Albert Hall. In Hyde Park proper, across Knightsbridge, is the Albert Memorial. As we drove by, I remembered the Arab Hall in Leighton House, just behind the Victoria and Albert Museum. Its tiled pool and exotic art, including *Young Athlete with Python,* speak of an earlier fascination with the Arab world that may have led to our problems today.

I pulled up in front of Jim's house on fashionable Drayton Gardens. A gray drizzle was falling on the calm wealth of elegant tree-lined Kensington. Just behind us a beat-up pale blue Ford pulled up. In the mirror I saw the skinhead and Jenny.

The east side of Bedford Square in 1851, before Virginia Woolf made it fashionably unfashionable to live in the area.

"Out," ordered the Arab.

"You might get a ticket here. It would be tough luck if you got clamped."

"I said out." Around the edges of the sunglasses, his eyes wrinkled menacingly.

We got out. With the Arab, I walked up and rang Jim's buzzer. Then I took a moment to turn around. Through the window of the car, I could make out Jenny, though I couldn't see her face, only inches from the monster. What were they talking about?

Jim answered the door in his bathrobe and pajamas.

"John," he exclaimed. "What a surprise." But when his eyes took in the Arab, his face grew taut. The Arab produced his gun, turned, and whistled. I heard car doors open and slam closed again, as the skinhead and Jenny got out of the car. They walked up the steps to join us at the door.

"I'm sorry, Jim," I said. "They want that bag."

"The bag? I'll get it."

"No!" said the Arab. "First we go in, everyone."

We had little choice but to enter. Inside, Jim's flat was dark and cold—neither the English nor the Scottish make unnecessary use of lights or heat. I have heard often the argument that central heating causes colds. However, none of this sat well with the Arab.

"Turn some lights on! We can't do business in the dark. And turn on the heat. This is barbarous."

"It's not cold," said Jim. "And you can see."

"Just turn on the heat," yelled the Arab. "And the lights." In

164

the light, I looked at Jenny, tired, eyes glowing bright.

"Where's the bag?" demanded the Arab.

"I was going to get it," said Jim.

"Do so," said the Arab, brandishing the gun.

"If you'd like to wait in the living room," offered Jim.

"Yes. The living room!" said the Arab. "Everyone in."

Jim's living room was Spartan but comfortable, with two large wing chairs and a sofa in front of a large bay window decorated with sheer white curtains. A braided oval rug covered most of the floor. We all sat down. The Arab amused himself by looking at the framed newspaper stories that hung over the mantelpiece.

A moment later Jim returned with the bag. "Here it is."

"Good."

"Untie Ms. Wilde," said the Arab to Wendell.

"What?"

"I said untie Ms. Wilde."

The skinhead began to make an unhappy whimpering noise.

"You heard me, you half-wit."

Reluctantly, the monster complied.

"Now, let us make sure everything is here." He brought the satchel up to the sofa. Laying his gun on the small table in front, he opened the bag. He brought out the clothing, then, ripping hard, the false bottom. At last, he slowly produced a piece of tissue paper. Unwrapping it, he held up a pair of gold earrings, two snakes devouring themselves.

"Do you see what treasures you've had under your noses?" he laughed at me and Jim.

Jim snorted.

The Arab reached into the satchel again, removing another piece of tissue. He unwrapped it to reveal a small earthenware cup, then smiled brightly.

"Four-thousand years ago, during the reign of Amenhotep, a princess drank from this cup." He stared at Jim. "Have you ever possessed such treasures in your house? I doubt it." He reached in again. This time he produced a carved ivory bangle, decorated with flattened crocodiles.

"Mohammed, may I see?" asked Jenny. "For old time's sake?"

165

"May you see? Now that we have them back, why not?" He smiled beatifically.

Digging in again, Ali produced an elaborate, many-stringed necklace of turquoise-colored faience. "Of the finest faience and carnelian. From Karnak, I should guess. The XVIII dynasty."

Jenny walked across the room and bent down.

"Yes, my dear!" continued the Arab. "It would have been a shame to have killed you. I am doubly glad to have recovered this treasure." He pressed the necklace up to her breast, holding it against her tweed jacket. "It becomes you."

"Do you have to tell me that?" She moved close and, in an instant, had the gun from the table. Holding it with both hands, she pointed it into his face.

"You bastard. I ought to shoot you now."

The Arab lunged, missed. Jenny retrained the gun on his head. His sunglasses had fallen off. He reached down to get them, and I noticed then that his eyes were blue. He put his glasses back on.

"Now, shall we call the police?" Jenny asked me. "The only problem is, John, you'll have to do it. I'm afraid they may not be in favor of my cause." She laughed nervously.

Still holding the gun with two hands, Jenny directed the Arab and Wendell away from the satchel and into the far corner near the fireplace. Then she stooped to put the loot back in the bag. "Where's the phone?" she asked.

"In the bedroom," answered Jim.

Suddenly, Wendell made a move for the window.

"Stop!" yelled Jenny, as she ran after him. He turned, realized he'd been caught, and made a whimpering noise.

"You thought you'd get away, you dog?" she yelled. "Back in the corner."

"Jenny!" I yelled. She turned. It was too late. The Arab was gone. A moment later we heard a motor turn over and a car squealing down the street.

"I can't believe it," said Jenny. "He's gone."

"I have his license plate number."

"Oh, John!" Jenny sighed.

"Let me see the gun," I said.

"See the gun?" asked Jenny. "Why? What's the matter?"

"Let me see it," I said again.

I reached over and took it from her.

"Of course. What's the matter?" she smiled. I walked back to the door, where Jim stood impassively.

"Jim, call the police," I said. He nodded.

"Good idea, John. Only in that case, I better be going," said Jenny.

Suddenly, an awful noise, something between a yelp and a growl, came from the corner. The skinhead was barking and twisting his head back and forth.

"You're not going to give me o'er to them," he screamed.

"Oh, yes, we are," laughed Jenny.

"Noooooo!" he yelled, as he charged past Jenny, past me, and right into Jim, who, after a brief struggle, had him in a full Nelson.

"No!" yelled the skinhead.

"Jenny's right. We're going to turn you over to the police," I said. He began to whimper again, a slobbering cry. Jim released him, and he fell into a chair.

Jenny smiled.

"And you, too, Jenny." I pointed the gun at her.

"What?" she laughed. She looked down at her feet, then around the room—at the window, the door, then back at me. I think she was surprised to see that I was still standing there pointing a gun at her.

"John? You're not serious."

"Jim, the cops."

"Right." He turned and went to call the police, closing the door behind him.

"Really, John, I have to be going now before they get here. Didn't you see what they did to me? What's the matter with you, John?"

"Not yet. You're not going yet. Not until we've done some talking." I had to get the truth from her. Even if it meant giving up all the dreams I'd had of her. My instincts as a reporter took over. I had to know. And it seemed this would be my last chance to find out.

"What? What do you mean, John? John, may I have my gun back?"

167

Jim came back from the other room. "On their way."

"OK, the police will be here any minute."

She stared at me. And then, suddenly, she broke down in tears. I resisted going over to comfort her.

"John," she cried. "John, can't I talk to you? Can't I at least talk to you?"

"Talk."

She sniffled. "Not here. Alone."

"All right." I handed Jim the gun. "Let's go." We went into Jim's bedroom.

"Go ahead," I said.

"Well...well, John, you saw. What they did to me. And, John, I have to go before they get here, the police. And."

"What?"

"That's it."

"If you won't talk, I'll talk for you. You gave me a suitcase full of antiquities, but not the real ones. No. If they were real, the Arab would never have left without them. Is that right? Those baubles you gave me are fake, as fake as the ones you wear, as fake as the ones they sell in the shop of the British Museum."

"John, that's not true. Or, if it is true, what does it matter?"

"I have a feeling there are a lot of those fake antiquities floating around. Your people do a good job with those fakes. And why shouldn't they? The people who made the originals in Egypt, their descendants, hundreds of generations later, make the fakes. That drinking cup out in the other room comes from the same mud as the real one, only three millennia later. I have a feeling you had a plan to use them in the British Museum itself, replacing real things with these fakes. Only the numbers are real, I remember you said. Not that I care. The whole museum could be fake for all I care. You're right. The British stole them from Egypt, and now you're stealing them back. But I draw the line at being played for a sucker."

"John. Stop. No. This isn't true."

"Because I was stupid enough to fall in love you, stupid enough to believe those eyes, those kisses, those lips meant something, I went along with your plan."

"You can't say that. They wanted to hurt you. I didn't."

"To begin with, the antiquities weren't stolen from Lord Prescott's until the day before the auction. I was there. I can see the ones in the bag correspond, but I've had that bag almost a month."

"What difference does it make?"

"It was a coincidence, all right, that we had the same initials. The plan, though, was not for me to transport a bag, but for me to get caught with one. After the Arab and Wendell had escaped, you planned to leave me with the bag to explain to the police. Not knowing the treasures were fake, the police would have taken me in. I may be stupid, but I'm not that stupid. Who is the Arab? Your boyfriend? Fess up."

"No," she began to tear.

"Who is he? Tell me! Is he your boyfriend or just your boss?"

"No. He's my...bbb..."

"Go on, say it. Your boyfriend."

"My brother."

I stared at her, as she continued to cry.

"You see, my father, our father, was quite a...rake in Cairo. With all the Egyptian women on his digs. We had different mothers but one father—you can tell from our eyes. I didn't want to frame you. That was his idea. He doesn't like Americans. We thought that if they got the fakes back, they wouldn't know the difference—at least not until we had had a chance to get the real pieces out of the country. They would have to use carbon 14 to determine the authenticity of the treasures, and that would take time.

"What I said about wanting to return those things to Egypt was true. That's my mission. That's my life. I didn't want to harm you, John. The police...the police would have believed your story. They would have believed it, and you would have been free. And we would have been free to continue collecting the antiquities."

My mind was spinning like a top. I was doing everything I could not to believe her.

"At first, I didn't care. So you got caught. But then after I'd spent time with you. It was so funny—that time you fell in the mud, you looked so...I couldn't help but feel something for you. And that night at dinner at your hotel. And then I didn't want you to know that I had betrayed you. It was my idea for them to tie me up. And, John, I'm so sorry. But the pieces were fake. So you wouldn't have gotten in trouble."

"Get up," I said.

"What?"

"Get up." She rose.

"No, John, please don't turn me over. If you do, I'll never get out of jail. That's worse than what I've done to you. To send me to jail for so long. For what?"

"C'mon." I opened the bedroom door, and we walked back into the living room.

"Get up," I said to the skinhead.

He bared his teeth, but he stood up.

"Now, both of you, beat it!"

Jenny stared at me.

"You heard me. Before I change my mind. The police'll be here any minute. Hurry. I think we can count on Jim to be quiet." I looked over at my friend. He nodded.

"Did you hear me? Beat it." Jenny looked at me and then at Wendell, who sort of bowed to me, made a slight bark, and then sprinted toward the door. We heard him scurry down the steps, and a moment later his car squealed off. Jenny turned to follow.

"Jenny," I said. She stopped. I handed her the gun, which she took. "Now go on. Quickly."

She nodded. At the door, she turned once more, eyes teary and blue.

"Well?" I said.

"Goodbye, John."

"Goodbye."

She lingered an instant, then hurried out the door. A moment later I heard a car pull up, doors slam, and then the ring of the bell. The police.

"We got a report from your hotel that something was fishy, but by the time we arrived, you were gone," the puffing inspector explained, removing his hat and rubbing his shoes on the mat. None other than Bosdale and a uniformed bobby.

"Take a look," I said. "The stolen treasures, or so it seems. You'll have to do tests, of course, carbon 14 and so on, to tell if they're real."

"My god, if they are, they're worth a fortune," said the inspector. He walked over and picked up the earrings. "Goodness gracious," he said. He wrapped up the earrings and returned them to the bag. "But what happened?"

I proceeded to tell the inspector a story—not entirely the true story. I left out the parts about my knowing Jenny and about my taking possession of the gun. In my story to Bosdale, the woman kept the gun. The Arab and Wendell fled the woman—whom I didn't name—while she was calling the police.

"Go easy on her if you catch her. She saved my life and left these valuables."

"Well, you've solved something of a caper, Mr. Woods. Are you going to write it up, or is Mr. MacAllister here to have that pleasure?" laughed Bosdale.

"Probably neither of us—not for a while anyway."

"Well you must be glad it's all over, dealing with people like that. We'll try and round them up, but they're a slippery lot. Anyway, they're out of your life, something to be glad of."

"That's true."

"Something wrong, Mr. Woods?"

My eyes moved over the room. I stared through the gauze curtains to the street. Then my eyes fell on Jim.

"John, what you need is a good whiskey," pronounced the Scotsman.

"Yes," I said. "That sounds like the thing. A whiskey."

* * *

To wrap up the guidebook part of this endeavor, I'd like to take you on a few day trips from London (I'm ready to get out of the city for a while).

Day trips from London

Rail and coach services link London to most places in the country. Each of the capital's eight main train stations deals with a different region of the country—so make sure you are leaving from the right station. The system-wide British Rail Passenger Network Map is detailed and helpful. It is available at many train stations in Britain and from **BritRail Travel International** in New York, *(212)599-5400.*

Buses are less expensive than trains and a good way to see the country if you are on a budget.

Following are the approximate journey times from London by rail and/or coach to popular destinations.

- Arundel can be reached by train in 80 minutes.
- Bath can be reached by train in 75 minutes, by coach in 180 minutes.
- Blenheim Palace can be reached by coach in 120 minutes.
- Brighton can be reached by train in 52 minutes, by coach in 105 minutes.
- The Broadlands can be reached by train in 82 minutes (via Southampton).
- Canterbury can be reached by train in 80 minutes, by coach in 105 minutes.
- Chichester can be reached by train in 98 minutes, by coach in 195 minutes.
- Dover can be reached by train in 87 minutes, by coach in 130 minutes.
- The Fishbourne Roman Palace can be reached by train in 101 minutes (via Chichester).
- Hampton Court Palace can be reached by train in 32 minutes, by coach in 57 minutes.
- Hastings can be reached by train in 105 minutes, by coach in 150 minutes.
- Hatfield House can be reached by train in 22 minutes, by coach in 62 minutes.
- Knebworth House can be reached by train in 34 minutes, by coach in 85 minutes.
- Leeds Castle can be reached by train (to Maidstone) in 53 minutes.
- Luton Hoo can be reached by train in 30 minutes, by coach in 62 minutes.
- Margate can be reached by train in 95 minutes, by coach in 135 minutes.
- Oxford can be reached by train in 45 minutes, by coach in 100 minutes.
- Rochester can be reached by train in 53 minutes, by coach in 80 minutes.
- Romney, Hythe & Dymchurch Railway along the English Channel can be reached by train in 75 minutes, by coach (to Folkestone) in 150 minutes.

• Rye can be reached by train in 97 minutes, by coach in 150 minutes.

• St. Albans can be reached by train in 18 minutes, by coach in 56 minutes.

• Stratford-upon-Avon can be reached by train in 146 minutes, by coach in 195 minutes.

• Windsor Castle can be reached by train in 48 minutes, by coach in 71 minutes.

• Woburn Abbey can be reached by coach in 125 minutes (summer Sundays only).

What to see

Arundel
One of the finest castles in England is at the heart of this picturesque town. The fortress was built in the 11th century and restored in the 18th century. Also visit the 1,100-acre Arundel Park and the Wildfowl Reserve.

Battle
This town is near the site of the Battle of Hastings, where the Anglo-Saxons lost their land to William the Conqueror on Oct. 14, 1066. You can follow the trail through the battlefield. Also visit the ruins of the Battle Abbey, founded by William the Conqueror in gratitude for his victory on the site over Harold Godwineson. (The high altar of the church is said to have been built over the spot on which Harold was killed.) Parts of the Battle Abbey were added in the 13th century.

Cambridge
A serene, pretty town, Cambridge is to Oxford as Yale is to Harvard. The magnificent architecture of Cambridge and the beauty of the surrounding countryside are reasons enough to spend several days here.

Cambridge was an early Roman site, initially a bridge or crossing over the

The University of Cambridge.

173

River Cam. At the time of the Domesday Book (1086), Cambridge was a small trading village. Scholars gathered here in 1209 after being ousted from Oxford by irate townspeople. They began a series of colleges that eventually became the university.

The lovely old city (in Britain, any town with a cathedral is called a city) did not always see eye to eye with the university, and riots took place in 1381. The phrase "town and gown" indicates some of the old animosity between the two.

King's College is one of the greatest Gothic structures in England. Trinity is the largest college in Cambridge, founded by Henry VIII in 1546. The Round Church, built in 1130, is one of the few surviving medieval circular churches. Queen's College is charming, appearing much as it did in the 15th century, when it was founded.

Canterbury

St. Augustine established Christianity here in A.D. 597, and in 1170 the martyr Thomas à Becket was murdered in the cathedral. Canterbury has been a settlement since the Iron Age. Visit the Canterbury Cathedral, the mother church for the Anglican faith and a center for pilgrimages. The structure was begun in 1070 and completed in 1503.

Dover

Known for its white cliffs, Dover was settled during the Iron Age. A massive 12th-century fortress is the leading attraction. Also visit the Pharos, a Roman lighthouse erected about A.D. 50. Take a stroll along the Marine Parade and the Prince of Wales and Admiralty piers. Visit the Roman Painted House on New Street; this second-century ruin has beautiful painted walls.

Ely

The subject of Anglo-Saxon folklore, Ely was once an island surrounded by the marshy, eel-inhabited Fens. An abbey was founded here in A.D. 673 and destroyed in A.D. 870, when the town was sacked by the Danes. Hereward the Wake, known as the "last of the English," defended the island against William the Conqueror until 1071. Ely Cathedral was built in 1083 on the site of the seventh-century St. Etheldreda's Abbey. In the 17th century, the Fens were drained, and Ely became a prosperous market town. Oliver Cromwell lived in the timbered house next to St. Mary's Church.

The Isle of Wight

The Old Village in Shanklin is charming, just what you imagine an English village should be. Thatched-roof cottages, many of them restaurants, pubs, and gift shops, line the streets. See St. Blasius, the old parish church, which dates in part from the 14th century. Climb down into the Shanklin Chine, a narrow ravine with a waterfall. The Isle of Wight is accessible from the mainland by hovercraft or ferry from Portsmouth or Southampton.

Knole House

This is one of England's largest and stateliest homes. The building was begun by Thomas Bouchier, archbishop of Canterbury, in the mid-15th century. It remained a palace for archbishops until it was appropriated by Henry VIII. Since 1566, the descendants of Thomas Sackville have lived here, including the novelist and gardener Vita Sackville-West and her husband Harold Nicolson, the diplomat and writer. Also see the nearby Ightham Mote, an early 14th-century moated manor house.

Oxford

Oxford University, with its 34 colleges and thousands of students, draws visitors from around the world. The famous Magdalen deer can be spotted in the private deer park at Magdalen College (pronounced Maudlen), built in the 15th century. Magdalen has more than 100 acres, which include, in addition to the deer park, lawns, gardens, and water walks.

New College isn't new at all—it was built in the late 14th century. It has a medieval cloisters and peaceful gardens. You can see a section of the old city walls here.

While the university was founded in the 12th century, the town itself dates back to A.D. 912. Fans of Dorothy Sayers have a special reason to visit the historic city. The hero of many of her mystery stories, Sir Peter Wimsey, hails from Oxford, and several of her books take place in the university town (including G*audy Night*).

The oldest public museum in Britain, the Ashmolean, is in Oxford. Here you can see works by Renaissance artists Raphael and Michelangelo, as well as works by Dutch masters and French impressionists. The Ashmolean also contains historic curios, such as the lantern Guy Fawkes carried when he tried to blow up Parliament in 1605.

The place to stay in Oxford is the Bear Inn. This establishment, seven centuries old, has oak beams and low ceilings. Rooms on the upper stories have sloping floors, and the steps are uneven. The Bear Inn is an important part of Oxford College tradition; students meet here to sing university songs and hold parties. The inn is also known for its extensive collection of ties. More than 4,200 neckties, donated by customers since 1951, hang on the walls here. Each one is tagged with the owner's signature. The collection includes ties from members of rowing clubs, cricket teams, student societies, and Olympic teams. They are organized according to the nationalities of their owners.

Rochester

This ancient cathedral town's most famous resident was Charles Dickens, who not only lived here, but set many of his stories here as well. A museum explores his life and works. Also in Rochester are a Norman castle, a 12th-century cathedral, and a Roman wall.

Salisbury and Stonehenge

Ten miles outside the cathedral city of Salisbury is a circle of massive standing stones known as Stonehenge. Bus service is available from Salisbury to the ancient temple. Erected in several stages between the late Neolithic and the middle Bronze ages, Stonehenge is a mystery; no one is sure exactly how the huge rocks were placed here. Study up on Stonehenge before you visit—otherwise it may look like nothing more than a pile of rocks. And visit early, before the crowds arrive.

Stratford-upon-Avon

This theater town was the birthplace of William Shakespeare. Many of the buildings with which he was associated have been preserved and are open to the public. The Royal Shakespeare Theater is located on the River Avon. "The Shakespeare Connection," a tour of the area by train and bus, departs London's Euston Station every morning.

Winchester

Winchester, the first capital of England and an ancient seat of learning, is one of England's most elegant and beautiful towns, with cobblestoned streets and good antique shops. Winchester's history goes back to the Iron Age, when the town was settled by the Celts. Later it became a Roman center. Winchester Cathedral, one of the largest in Europe, was begun in 1079 on the site of earlier Saxon churches.

Windsor

Located on the River Thames, Windsor is a picturesque Victorian town. Windsor Castle, still used by royalty after 850 years, attracts thousands of visitors. The castle was begun by William the Conqueror in the 11th century and is the largest inhabited castle in the world. Many of Britain's kings and queens are buried in St. George's Chapel.

Across the Thames from Windsor is Eton College, the exclusive boys' school founded in 1440. Eton has educated many of the nation's leaders.

For more information on these and other day trips from the city, consult *Day Trips from London* by Earl Steinbicker (Hastings House Publishers, New York).

Chapter XII

The MI5 man grilled me again later that day, but I survived it without naming Jenny. Claridge's apologized for the mishap and made more than suitable amends.

I continued my rounds, moving to a lovely room at the Connaught, complete with an open fireplace and a view of Carlos Place. A few days after I had checked in, Jim and Nigel stopped by to join me for a drink in the Connaught's comfortable bar (where famed barman Tony set them up for us).

"You have a true talent for drama," said Nigel. "You seem to prove Wilde's theory that life imitates art."

"That girl was a work of art," pronounced Jim.

"I wish I'd seen her," said Nigel. "But there's one thing I don't understand. You say you met this girl thanks to a writer friend of yours, a William Chamberlayne. Did he know anything about her? I mean, was he involved in this, too?"

"I wouldn't be surprised if William had something of an inkling that there was more to this woman than met the eye. That's just what would have piqued his curiosity. I know he planned on writing this book himself. He's the type that looks for adventure. He made me his guinea pig."

"I don't know if I'd be grateful or angry," said Nigel.

"There was something to be grateful about with that Jenny Wilde," said Jim, winking.

"That's life. Maybe we'll meet again—although I doubt it."

"What is it that Puck says?" wondered Nigel. "'If we shadows have offended, think but this, and all is mended. That you have but slumb'red here. While these visions did appear.'"

"Thanks, Nigel," I said. "Let me buy you a drink."

Index

10 Downing St., 87
American Express, 7-8
Arundel, 173
Bank of England, 91, 96
Banquet House, 87
Barclay's, 8
Battle, 173
Bed and breakfasts, 29
Belgravia, 135
Bicycles, 21
Big Ben, 86-87
Bloomsbury, 27-28, 104
British Air, 2
British Rail, 18
British Travel Center, 13
BritRail Travel International, 171
Buses, 15, 19
    Victoria Coach Station, 15
Cambridge, 173-174
Camden Jazz Festival, 139
Canterbury, 174
Carlyle, John, 95
Chelsea, 104-105
Christie's, 147-148
Churches
    St. Alfege's Church, 110
    St. Bartholomew-the-Great, 94
    St. James's, 94
    St. Martin-in-the-Fields, 94
    St. Paul's Cathedral, 43, 90, 94
    Westminster Abbey, 83-86, 95
    Westminster Cathedral, 95
Cinemas
    Curzon, 121
    Everyman Cinema, 121
    Institute of Contemporary
      Art, 121-122
    National Film Theatre, 122
    Roxie Cinema Club, 122
City, The, 105

Covent Garden, 42-44, 105
Currency, 7-8
Dickens, Charles, 27, 95-95
Docklands, 109
Dover, 174
Driving, 20-21
    Car parks, 20
    Car rentals, 21
Electric current, 8-9
Ely, 174
Embassies and high
    commissions, 12-13
Emergency information, 12
English National Opera, 120
Federal Express, 11
Ferries, 17
    Sealink, 17
Fire, 91, 154
Fleet Street, 105-106
Galleries
    Courtauld Institute
      Galleries, 27, 93
    Institute of Contemporary
      Arts, 93
    National Gallery, 87, 93
    National Portrait
      Gallery, 87-88, 93
    South Banks Arts Complex, 94
    Tate Gallery, 94
    Wallace Collection, 94
Greenwich, 110-112
Guildhall, 92
Hampstead, 106
Haymarket, 6
Heathrow airport, 2-3
History of the city, 153-156
Hotels
    Alexander, 32
    Athenaeum, 34
    Basil Street Hotel, 33

Berners, 30-31
Blakes, 32
Brown's, 34
Capital Hotel, 33
Claridge's, 34-35, 123
Connaught, 35
Dukes Hotel, 35
Durrants, 34
Ebury Court, 37
Fielding, 31
Goring Hotel, 37
Grosvenor House, 35
Hyde Park, 33
Inn on the Park, 35
Inverness Court, 31
Meridien Piccadilly, 35-36
Number Sixteen, 32
Park Lane, 36
Portobello Hotel, 30
Ritz, 4, 36
Savoy, 31
Stafford, 36-37
Swiss Cottage Hotel, 32
Vicarage, 32-33
Waldorf, 31-32
Wansbeck, 31
Westbury, 37
Wilbraham, 33-34
Inns of Court, 96-97
Isle of Wight, 175
Johnson, Dr. Samuel, 96
Keats, John, 96
Kensington, 106
Knole House, 175
London University, 28
Mall, The, 107
Mayfair, 107
Monument, 97
Mopeds and motorcycles, 21
Museums
    British Museum, 7, 23-27, 99
    Geological Museum, 99
    Imperial War Museum, 100
    John Soane Museum, 28, 101
    London Toy and Model
      Museum, 100
    Madame Tussaud's, 100
    Museum of London, 100
    Museum of Mankind, 100
    Museum of the Moving
      Image, 100
    National Maritime
      Museum, 110, 112
    Natural History Museum, 100
    Old Royal
      Observatory, 110, 112
    Percival-Davis Foundation of
      Chinese Art, 28
    Pollock's Toy Museum and
      Shop, 28
    Science Museum, 100-101
    Theatre Museum, 43, 101
    Transport Museum, 43, 100
    Victoria and Albert
      Museum, 101
Nightclubs
    100 Club, 139
    Annabel's, 140
    Camden Palace, 140
    Comedy Store, 140
    Hippodrome, 140
    Marquee, 140
    Pizza Express, 139
    Pizza on the Park, 139
    Raymond's Revue Bar, 142
    Rock Garden, 140
    Ronnie Scott's, 139
    Stringfellow's, 140
    Wat, 141
Old Bailey, 97
Oxford, 175-176
Palaces
    Buckingham Palace, 101
    Kensington Palace, 101
    Lambeth Palace, 102
    St. James's Palace, 60-61, 102
Parks
    Hampstead Heath, 102-103
    Hyde Park, 103
    Kensington Gardens, 103
    Kew Gardens, 152
    Regent's Park, 104
    St. George's Gardens, 104
    St. James's Park, 104, 138
    Victoria Tower Gardens, 104
Parliament, 86, 97-98
Piccadilly, 6, 107
Plague, 91, 154

Postal Service, 11
Pubs
   Audley, 131
   Cheshire Cheese, 131
   El Vino's, 131
   Lamb and Flag, 131
   Marquess of Anglesea, 131
   Museum Tavern, 131
   Nag's Head, 132
Regent Street, 6
Restaurants
   Amico, 56
   Bibendum, 50
   Blooms, 50
   Bombay Brasserie, 50
   Boulestin, 47
   Café des Amis
      du Vin, 40-42, 47
   Café du Jardin, 47-48
   Café Pelican, 54
   Calabash, 48
   Connaught, 53
   Criterion Brasserie/Café, 54
   Dorchester, 53-54
   Drakes, 51
   Escargot, 54
   Food for Thought, 48
   Fortnum and Mason, 56
   Garrick, 112
   Gavvers, 51
   Gay Hussar, 55
   George & Vulture, 46-47
   Hard Rock Café, 52
   Harrods, 56
   Hobson's, 152
   Inigo Jones, 49
   Interlude de Taballiau, 49
   Joe's Café, 51
   Justin de Blank, 52-53
   Khan's, 46
   Langan's Brasserie, 53
   Le Gavroche, 53
   Le Papillon, 110
   Ma Cuisine, 51
   Maison Bouquillon, 56
   Meridien Piccadilly, 55-56
   Mrs. Stokes' Kitchen, 56-57
   Ménage à Trois, 52
   Nam Long, 55
   Nontas, 46
   Orations, 118
   Paper Tiger, 51
   Partridges, 57
   Rasa Sayang, 55
   Richoux, 62
   Ritz, 5-6, 53
   Rules, 49
   Savoy, 48-49
   Sea Shell, 52
   Simpson's-in-the-Strand, 49
   Soho Brasserie, 55
   Sweetings, 47
   Tante Claire, 51-52
   Villa Blanca, 50
Rochester, 176
Royal Albert Hall, 98
Royal Exchange, 91-92
Royal Naval College, 112
Royal Opera House, 120
Salisbury, 176
Scotland Yard, 87
Shopping
   Antiques
      Bermondsey Market, 64
      Camden Passage, 64
      Relcy Antiques, 110
   Books
      Cecil Court, 64
      Dillons, 64
      Foyles, 64-65
      Francis Edwards, 65
      Hatchards, 65
      Heywood Hill, 65
      J.A. Allen, 65
      Maggs Brothers
         Ltd., 65-66
      Samuel French Theatre
         Bookshop, 66
      W.H. Smith, 66
      Waterstones, 66
   Cheese
      Paxton & Whitfield, 66
   Department stores
      Fortnum and Mason, 66-67
      Harrods, 67-68, 133-135
      Liberty, 68
      Marks and Spencer, 68
      Peter Jones, 68

Selfridges, 68
Guns
    Holland & Holland, 69
    James Purdey & Sons, 69
    William Evans, 69
Hats
    James Lock & Company, 69-70
Perfume
    Floris & Company Perfumers, 70
Raincoats
    Aquascutum, 70
    Burberrys, 70
Shirts
    Harvie & Hudson, 71
    Sale Shop, 71
    Turnbull & Asser, 71
Shoes
    Blackman's Shoe Shop, 71
    Church's, 71
    John Lobbs, 71
    Trickers, 71
    Wildsmith, 72
Specialty shops
    Anything Left-Handed Ltd., 72
    Arthur Middleton, 72
    Asprey, 72
    Constant Sale Shop, 72
    Davenport's, 72
    General Trading Company, 72
    Hyper-Hyper, 73
    Irish Linen Company, 73
    Kite Store, 73
    Prestat, 73
    Reject China Shop, 73
    Savoy Taylors Guild, 73
    Sulka, 73
Sports
    Lillywhites, 73
Stationery
    Chisolm's, 73-74
    Falkiner's Fine Papers, 74
    Ryman, 74
    Smythson of Bond Street, 74

Street markets
    Bermondsey Market, 161
    Camden Lock, 161-162
    Camden Passage, 162
    Greenwich, 162 10
    Petticoat Lane, 162
    Portobello Road, 162
Suits
    Anderson & Sheppard, 75
    Blades of Savile Row, 75
    H. Huntsman & Sons, 75
    Kilgour, French & Stanbury Ltd., 75
    Paul Smith, 75
    Stovel & Mason Ltd., 75
    Tommy Nutter, 75-76
Sweaters
    Irish Shop, 76
    Portobello China & Woollens Ltd., 76
    Westaway & Westaway, 76
Tobacco
    Alfred Dunhill's, 76-77
    Robert Lewis, 77
Toys
    Hamleys, 77
Umbrellas
    James Smith & Sons, 77
    Swaine, Adeney, Briggs & Sons, 77
Wine
    Berry Brothers & Rudd Ltd., 78
    Green's, 78
    John Harvey & Sons Ltd., 78
    Oddbins, 78
Women's fashions
    Browns, 79
    Harvey Nichols, 79
    Laura Ashley, 79
    Liberty of London, 79
    Marks and Spencer, 79-80
    Rayne, 80
    Sheepskin Shop, 80
Shopping districts
    Fulham Road, 80-81

Kensington Church Walk, 81
Mayfair, 81-82
South Molton Street, 82
St. James's, 82
Soho, 107-108, 141-142
Speakers' Corner, 126-127
Sports
   Cricket, 142
   Equestrian events, 142
   Football, 143
   Rowing, 143
   Rugby, 143-144
   Swimming, 144-145
      Berkeley Hotel, 144
      Champneys Health
         Club, 144
      Crystal Palace National
         Sports Centre, 144
      Fitness Centre, 144-145
      Highgate Pond, 145
      Kenwood Ladies'
         Pond, 145
      Oasis, 145
      Porchester Baths, 145
      Serpentine Lido, 145
      YMCA, 145
   Tennis, 145
Stonehenge, 176
Stratford-upon-Avon, 176
Taxis, 19-20
Telegrams, 11
Telephones, 9-11
Thames River, 88
Theater tickets, 114-116
   Exchange Travel, 114
   First Call, 114
   Keith Prowse &
      Company, 114-115
   Obtainables Ltd., 115
   Sidi, 115
   Ticketmaster, 115
Theaters
   Barbican Centre, 117-118
   Bush Theatre, 120
   Cabaret Mechanical Theatre, 43
   Donmar Warehouse, 120
   Duke of York's Theatre, 119
   Holland Park Open Air
      Theater, 119

Institute of Contemporary Arts
   Theatre, 120
London Coliseum, 120
Mermaid Theatre, 120
Old Vic, 118
Royal Court Theater, 118-119
Sadler's Wells Theatre, 121
South Bank Arts Complex, 118
Young Vic, 118
Thomas Cook, 8
Tipping, 9
Tourist Information Centre, 13
Tower of London, 92, 98-99
Trafalgar Square, 6, 108
Train travel
   Charing Cross Station, 15
   Euston Station, 15
   King's Cross Station, 15
   Liverpool Street Station, 15
   Paddington Station, 15
   St. Pancras Station, 15
   Victoria Station, 15
   Waterloo Station, 15
Underground, 17-18
Victoria Gardens, 86
Whitehall, 87, 99
Winchester, 176-177
Windsor, 177
Wine bars
   Brahms and Liszt, 132
   Coconut Grove, 132
   Dorchester, 132
   Ebury Wine Bar, 132
   Peppermint Park, 132
   Pheasantry, 132
Woolf, Virginia, 27